Jesus said the church is his body,
that he is the life of the body. "There
is one body and one Spirit, just
as you were called to the one hope that
belongs to your call, one Lord,
one faith, one baptism, one God and
Father of us all, who is above all and
through all and in all."

But in many places today it seems
the life has gone out of the body.

In the early church all Christians
were intimately and actively involved in the
vibrant life of the body. Their witness
to unbelievers coupled with their
deep love for each other rocked the
Roman world. And it must be so again.

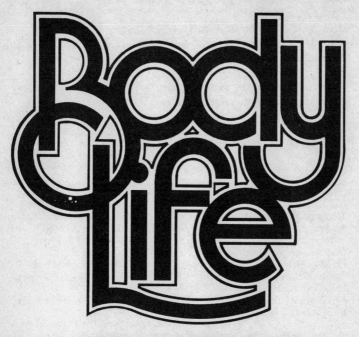

RAY C. STEDMAN

Regal
Books
A Division of GL Publications
Ventura, CA 93006

Other good reading by Ray C. Stedman:
Folk Psalms of Faith
Highlights of the Bible: Genesis—Nehemiah
What More Can God Say?
Highlights of the Bible: Poets and Prophets

For information on the author's Discovery Series, contact Discovery Foundation, Palo Alto, California 94306.

The foreign language publishing of all Regal books is under the direction of GLINT. GLINT provides financial and technical help for the adaptation, translation and publishing of books in more than 85 languages for millions of people worldwide.

For more information write: GLINT, Ventura, California 93006.

The Scripture quotations in this publication, unless otherwise indicated, are from the *Revised Standard Version* of the Bible, copyrighted 1946 and 1952 by the Division of Christian Education of the NCCC, U.S.A., and used by permission. Other versions quoted include:
Phillips, THE NEW TESTAMENT IN MODERN ENGLISH, Revised Edition, J.B. Phillips, Translator. © J.B. Phillips 1958, 1960, 1972. Used by permission of Macmillan Publishing Co., Inc.
NIV, New International Version, New Testament. Copyright © 1973 by New York Bible Society International. Used by permission.
NEB from *The New English Bible.* © The Delegates of the Oxford University Press and The Syndics of the Cambridge University Press 1961, 1970. Reprinted by permission.
KJV Authorized King James Version

© Copyright 1972 by Ray C. Stedman
All rights reserved

Thirteenth Printing, 1981

Published by
Regal Books
A Division of GL Publications
Ventura, California 93006
Printed in U.S.A.

Library of Congress Catalog Card No. 74-181764

ISBN 0-8307-0732-8

Second Edition Revised, 1977
Third Edition, 1979

Photos by Bob Bebb, John McElroy, Roger Murray, Ron Widman.

Contents

A Study Guide for leader and student
is available for this book from your
church supplier.

Foreword

Much is being said today about the church being irrelevant. With many observers of the religious scene the church has become the whipping-boy for many of the world's ills.

It depends, of course, on how one defines the "church." In *Body Life* Ray C. Stedman uses the leverage of the Word itself to bring us back to the church's real meaning and mission. With strong, convincing argument he points to the weaknesses within the institutional church, and clearly reminds us of the strength inherent in Christ's body, the true church.

This book is not all theory and semantics. In chapter twelve the author relates how his interpretation of the church has worked effectively in the crucible of practical experience. He convinces us that the New Testament definition of the church is the outworking of Christ Jesus through his corporate Body.

His Peninsula Bible Church began with only five laymen who felt the need for more meaningful and effective Christian witness, and a richer "koinonia" than
they were accustomed to. These five, convinced that
the church too often boxed itself behind stone walls,
took the church to the people of their community with
sincerity, dedication, and effectiveness. Today, it is one
of the most dynamic company of Christian believers on
the West Coast.

Ray C. Stedman, eager to share Peninsula's blessings
with other groups, has given us in *Body Life* a "how-
to" book which shows us how the church can relate to
community life in a meaningful, satisfactory, and redeeming manner.

Billy Graham

CHAPTER ONE

The Most Powerful Force on Earth

This book is about the church. Not the church as it often is, but the church as it originally was and can be—yes, must be—again. The word "church" conjures up many widely differing images. To some, the church is nothing but a snooty religious country club with traditional rituals as sacred as those at a fox hunt. To others the church is a political action group, a pressure bloc of do-gooders, waging battle against social ills. Some see the church as a kind of nonsegregated waiting room for people expecting to take the next bus for heaven. Some view it as a kind of a low calorie dessert for any who want something nice that won't hurt their public image. Others think of it as a regular meeting of religious hopheads enjoying their weekend religious jag. To many, the church is a kind of waterboy to the game

1

of life or a religious democracy trying to legislate morals for the rest of the world.

Let us be perfectly honest and admit that the church has often been all these things, at many times and places. It has amply justified every bitter charge leveled against it. Nevertheless, despite its many weaknesses and its tragic sins the church has been, in every century since its inception, the most powerful force for good on the face of the earth. It has been light in the midst of a darkness so dense it could be felt. It has been salt in society, retarding the spread of moral corruption and adding zest and flavor to human life.

Two Churches

How can this be? How can the same institution be at once the source of heartache, disillusionment and despair to many and the source of joy, life and endless comfort to many others? The answer of the Bible is that what we call the church is really two churches. Both are religious but one is selfish, power-hungry, cruel and devilish. The other is strong, loving, forgiving and godly. One has fomented human hatred and caused society to erupt in continual bloody conflicts, all done in the name of God and religion. The other has healed human hurt, broken down barriers of race and class and delivered men and women everywhere from fear, guilt, shame and ignorance. The latter is the true church, begun by Jesus Christ and manifesting authentic Christianity. The other is a false church, a satanic organization, a counterfeit Christianity.

Jesus himself is the one who predicted this would be the case. In Matthew 13, in an amazing series of parables in which he described the conditions that would prevail in the world during the age between his first and second comings (the present age in which we live) he gave what is frequently called the parable of the wheat and the tares. In the *Revised Standard Version,* the word for tares is translated *"weeds."* There he said that he, as the Son of Man, would sow wheat (true Christians whom he called the sons of the kingdom) in the field of the world. But while men were unaware the devil would come and sow weeds (false Christians called sons of the evil one) among the wheat. The two would grow up together, indistinguishable at first. Men would soon note, however, the weeds among the wheat and would come asking if they should dig up the weeds. His answer was clearly and positively, no! If that were attempted, he explained, the wheat would be destroyed along with the weeds. *Let both grow together until the harvest* (Matt. 13:30).

The harvest, he went on to explain, would be at the close of the age when he would send his angels (not men) into the field to separate the weeds from the wheat. The weeds would be burned in judgment, but wheat would be gathered into his father's barns. The wheat, sons of the kingdom, are those who have experienced what the Bible calls the new birth. In another place Jesus said clearly, *Unless one is born anew, he cannot see the kingdom of God* (John 3:3).

The apostle Peter later describes these as being *born anew, not of perishable seed but of imperishable, through the living and abiding word of God* (1 Pet. 1:23). The sons of the evil one are the false Christians, never born again by the power of the Spirit of God through faith in the Word of God, but who imagine they are Christians because they have fulfilled some certain ritual, have joined a local church or are relying on outward moral conduct or intense social concern for acceptance before God. To themselves and to many outside the church, they appear to be indistinguishable from the true Christians.

No wonder the church presents such a confused picture to the world. When the biblical picture is ignored (as it so often is) the church appears confusing even to those who love it and seek to defend it. Today the church seems to have lost its sense of identity. Like someone suffering from amnesia it is asking, "Who am I and what am I here for?" The attempt to view as one church two completely contradictory entities has produced a kind of ecclesiastical schizophrenia that has left many confused and baffled.

This dual character of the church has often been sensed by many and attempts have been made through the centuries to separate the true church from the false. But every such attempt has failed because the separation has been attempted on the basis of external factors. Doctrinal purity, moral conduct, ritualistic practice and state affiliation have been some of the varying measuring sticks by which the true church has been sought—and claimed! Roman Catholics have insisted they had the true church, Baptists have scorned such claims and declared they had the true pattern and others have said, "A plague on both your houses—we are the true church," and so the battle has raged for centuries.

Two-in-One Christians

The truth is, of course, that no religious organization or denomination is or can be the true church. The division does not lie along those lines. True Christianity cannot be separated out on the basis of groups or clusters of groups. It cannot even be separated by individuals. The biblical position is that though counterfeit Christians can only manifest counterfeit Christianity, true Christians are capable of displaying both true and false Christianity, though not at one and the same time. Whenever true Christians, through ignorance or willful disobedience, do display a false and counterfeit Chris-

4

tianity in their lives, they do as much harm to the world around them as if they were irreligious pagans living in utter selfishness and unconcern for others.

The sad but tragic truth is that it is quite possible to be a true Christian and yet not manifest true Christianity. It is deceptively easy to be a Christian yet not live a Christian life. The ironic thing is that that kind of Christian living is also dull, barren and deadly. Yet it is just as easy, so far as activity goes, to live a true Christian life which is always vital, exciting and effective.

The purpose of this book is to search out from the Scripture the nature and function of true Christianity and thus to recover the dynamic quality of early Christianity. Though life today seems terribly complicated by comparison, there is no reason why the church in the twentieth century should not be what it was in the first century. True Christianity operates now on exactly the same basis that it did then. The same dynamic impact described in the book of Acts is possible today.

The major factor that keeps this from happening today is ignorance. Most Christians are tragically unaware of the biblical pattern for the operation of the church. Even true Christians still try vainly to do what their Master forbade them (Matt. 13:24-30), to separate the weeds from the wheat in a physically isolated sense. They do not seem to realize that true and false Christianity can be intermingled in the same person. In such a case no physical separation is possible. To destroy one would be to destroy the other, as Jesus warned. In the biblical pattern, the wheat (true Christianity) should become so healthy and strong that it renders the weeds weak and sickly and thus virtually unable to carry out their noxious purpose.

Jesus declared that he would build his church upon a rock, an unshakeable foundation. That rock was the fact of his Messiahship and deity, as the apostle Peter

5

confessed. (Matt. 16:16) Subsequently, on the day of Pentecost, that church came into being by the power of the Spirit of God. At first there was no sign of the presence of false Christianity. The true Christian life which was displayed shook the entire city of Jerusalem and soon spread to other cities and villages. Then, as Jesus predicted, the false seeds of the devil's sowing took root and began to appear, not only as baptized but unregenerate members, but also as evil in the lives of true members of the church. (Acts 8, Simon Magus; Acts 5, Ananias and Sapphira.)

It then became the task of the apostles to instruct Christians in how to recognize the counterfeit life that was in them along with the true, how to repudiate the one in the power of a crucified Lord and to yield themselves by faith fully to Christ so that they might display the unique life of the resurrected and triumphant Lord. It was given to the apostles to develop in detail the pattern of operation intended by the Lord for his body, the church. This pattern, when closely followed, would make the church the most powerful force on earth in any age or time.

Undergirding Government

The amazing fact which Scripture clearly declares, but which thousands of Christians have failed to see, is that God has designed that his church should be a kind of government on earth undergirding visible governments. This would make possible a climate of benevolent law and order, the rule of justice and peace, and would hold in restraint the wild forces of tyranny, anarchy and murder. (See Matt. 5:13,14; Phil. 2:14,15; 1 Tim. 2:1,2.) Whenever the church has approached this biblical pattern, righteous conditions have begun to prevail. And when it has turned from this divine pattern to rely upon secondary forces it has either become proud, rich and tyrannical, or worldly, weak and despised by all.

The essential need then is that we should rediscover the biblical pattern. As one modern sign puts it—when all else fails, follow directions! When we turn back to the Scriptures we are returning to reality. There we come to the fundamental issue of any matter, to basic underlying truth from which we can work our way out again to apply to every area of life the great principles learned.

Though all the apostles who wrote the New Testament give us truth about the church, the primary writer in this respect is the apostle Paul. He devotes one entire letter (Ephesians) almost exclusively to the church, its origin, its nature, its function and its essential relationship to its Lord. To this letter we now turn, especially to the first sixteen verses of the fourth chapter. This will be our guideline to the truth about the church.

Where do I fit into the body?

CHAPTER TWO

The Church's Highest Priority

This is a revolutionary age. The hurricane winds of change are everywhere blowing. The race seethes with unrest and lawless rebellion. Staggering problems of social injustice, moral corruption and human cruelty confront the nations. What are Christians to do in this hour? What stance should the church take toward such complicated and entrenched problems? These are questions many are asking today.

When Paul wrote to the Christians in the city of Ephesus in the Roman province of Asia they were facing strikingly similar problems. Half the population of the Empire were slaves, sunk in a bondage so complete that they were traded and sold like so many cattle. Except for a small class of rich aristocrats and patricians, the other half of the population were tradesmen and laborers eking out a precarious living which was never far from poverty. The moral corruption of Ephesus was legendary. It was the center of worship for the sex-goddess, Diana of the Ephesians. And as for cruelty, the Roman legions were ready to march anywhere to suppress with ruthless slaughter the first sign of rebellion against the emperor's authority. That emperor was Nero, whose sordid and savage life was already the talk of the empire.

Paul was in Rome when he wrote, a prisoner of Caesar, awaiting the hour when he would be summoned before Nero. He was permitted to live in his own hired house but could not go about the city. He was chained day and night to a Roman guard. Seeing about him the decadent life of the city and knowing the conditions which prevailed in distant Ephesus, what would the apostle tell the Christians to do when he wrote? The answer is striking and pertinent:

I therefore, a prisoner for the Lord, beg you to lead a life worthy of the calling to which you have been called, with all lowliness and meekness, with patience, forbearing one another in love, eager to maintain the unity of the Spirit in the bond of peace (Eph. 4:1-3).

What does the apostle say to the church in Ephesus in the face of the desperate demands of human need? What is his answer to the cry for justice and relief arising from the lips of the oppressed citizens to whom he writes? Simply this: Fulfill your calling! Don't deviate from the divine strategy. Obey your orders. Follow your Head!

In this admonition the apostle clearly recognizes the true nature and function of the church. It is not a human institution. It is not expected to devise its own strategy and set its own goals. It is not an independent organization, existing by means of the strength of its numbers. It is, rather, a body called into a special relationship to God. Within this letter to the Ephesians,

9

the apostle employs several figures to describe the relationship. The church, he says, is a body under the control of its head. What a tragedy it would be if that body should refuse to respond to the direction of its head! The church is also a temple, for the exclusive habitation and use of a Person who dwells within and has the right to do with that temple whatever he wills. The church is an army under the command of a king. An army that will not obey its leader is useless as a fighting force. Therefore, says Paul to the church, obey your orders, follow your Head.

Behind Caesar

Paul himself is an example to them. After languishing for two years as a prisoner in Palestine (Caesarea), he had been sent to Rome on a very perilous sea voyage which ended in shipwreck on the island of Malta. But at long last he arrived at Rome. He was the personal prisoner of Nero, but never once in his letter does he refer to himself as "the prisoner of Caesar." It is always, as here, "a prisoner for the Lord," or "the prisoner of the Lord." He does not fret about being in prison, being chained and limited. Read his letter to the Philippians, also written from this prison, and you will find it is filled with joy and triumph and the assurance that all is well. To Paul, behind Caesar is Christ. He does not regard himself as a prisoner of Caesar because he sees beyond the chains and the guard and the imperial processes of justice the controlling hand of Jesus Christ.

In his letter to the Corinthians, Paul says, We look not to the things that are seen but to the things that are unseen (2 Cor. 4:18). Why? Because that is where the ultimate answers lie. That is where ultimate truth is found and ultimate power exists. Jesus himself reflected this same attitude when he stood before Pontius Pilate.

Pilate said to him, *Do you not know that I have power . . . to crucify you?* Jesus replied immediately, *You would have no power over me unless it had been given you from above* (John 19:10,11).

Much of the explanation for the confusion which exists so widely in the church today is that Christians have been looking at the things that are seen instead of at the things that are unseen. We see a suffering world with human need obvious everywhere. Hate and bigotry abound, injustice prevails and misery exists everywhere we turn. The obvious solution seems to be to marshal all our human resources to meet these needs. Let us get to work and do something about it—now! It sounds so logical, so consistent, so practical. But that is because our human thinking is shallow, superficial. We only see the things that are visible. In our shallow concern for externals we treat symptoms and not causes. We apply superficial remedies that work only for the moment, if they work at all, and then the situation is worse than it was before.

What is desperately needed today is this practical admonition of the apostle: *Lead a life worthy of the calling to which you have been called* (Eph. 4:1). The one who has called us sees life much more clearly than we do. He has devised a strategy that will actually remove the cause of human darkness and misery. He does not waste his time putting Band-Aids on cancer. He strikes right at the root cause. When the church is faithful to its calling it becomes a healing agency in society, able to lift a whole nation or an empire to a higher plateau of wholesome living. In his monumental history of the world, *The Story of Civilization,* Will Durant compares the influence of Caesar and Christ. He says of Jesus:

"The revolution he sought was a far deeper one,

11

without which reforms could be only superficial and transitory. If he could cleanse the human heart of selfish desire, cruelty, and lust, utopia would come of itself, and all those institutions that rise out of human greed and violence, and the consequent need for law, would disappear. Since this would be the profoundest of all revolutions, beside which all others would be mere *coup d'etats* of class ousting class and exploiting in its turn, Christ was, in this spiritual sense the greatest revolutionist in history."[1]

The true church is here to effect that revolution; the false church is here to oppose. But true Christians actually promote the cause of false Christianity when, through ignorance or mistaken zeal, they deviate from the divine strategy and do not obey their divine calling. We mere humans cannot improve on the divine program. Nor are we left in doubt as to what that calling is. The first three chapters of Ephesians are devoted to describing it; and it is found in many other places throughout the New Testament. If Christians are to give intelligent obedience to their Lord, they must give highest priority to understanding what it is he wants them to be and do. That divine calling is based upon fundamental and ultimate reality.

Back to Reality
That is the glory of Christianity—setting forth things as they really are. The characteristic of New Testament epistles is to begin with the truth, which is what we call doctrine. Then, on the basis of that underlying foundation of truth the writer goes on to suggest certain practical applications. How foolish it is to start with anything but truth! There are certain people

1. Will Durant, *The Story of Civilization Part III,* "Caesar and Christ" (New York: Simon and Schuster, 1944), p. 566.

12

today who tell us that we should start with some kind of a dream or an idealized hope. Building on that illusion, we are to work out practical solutions to our problems. But the apostles never do this. Each begins his writing with the truth, the truth as it is, with things as they actually exist. These writers call us back to reality.

In the opening chapters of Ephesians Paul gives several very clear statements of the purpose of the church: not merely its purpose for eternity someday but its purpose in time right now. Since Christians have in Christ far more than they had in their former condition in darkness and defeat in the kingdom of Satan, it is helpful to learn to what end and purpose this is all designed. Let us observe some of these statements of the nature and purpose of the church:

He chose us in him [Christ] *before the foundation of the world,* [the church is no afterthought with God. It was planned long before the world was made], *that we should be holy and blameless before him* (Eph. 1:4).

God's first concern is not what the church does, it is what the church *is*. Being must always precede doing, for what we do will be according to what we are. To understand the moral character of God's people is a primary essential in understanding the nature of the church. As Christians we are to be a moral example to the world, reflecting the character of Jesus Christ.

Recently I read of two American men who were riding on a train in Britain. (English trains have compartments where up to six people can be seated). In the compartment with these two men was a very distinguished-looking gentleman. The two Americans were quietly discussing him. In a very low tone one of them said, "I would wager money that he is the Archbishop of Canterbury."

The other man said, "I don't think so. I'll take your wager."

So the first man approached the gentleman and said, "Sir, would you mind telling us, are you the Archbishop of Canterbury?"

The man immediately replied, "Mind your own blankety-blank business. What the blankety-blank difference does it make to you?"

So the first American turned to the other and said, "The bet's off! There's no way of finding out!"

This story is but to suggest that Christians ought to be clearly evident by the way they talk and live, the way they act and react. We Christians are called to be "holy and blameless before him." That is one of the purposes of the church.

The Praise of His Glory

Paul gives us another purpose of the church in the first chapter of Ephesians:

He destined us in love to be his sons through Jesus Christ, according to the purpose of his will, to the praise of his glorious grace (v. 5).

We who first hoped in Christ have been destined and appointed to live for the praise of his glory (v. 12).

Think of that! *We who first hoped in Christ,* refers to us who are Christians as having been destined and appointed (here is our calling again) to live for the praise of his glory. The first task of the church is not the welfare of men, important as that may be and much as it definitely enters the picture. But it is not the church's first task. The first aim is to live to the praise and glory of God. As the *New English Bible* states it, "We should cause his glory to be praised."

What is God's glory? It is God himself, the revelation of what God is and does. The problem with this world is that it does not know God. It has no understanding of him. In all its seekings and wanderings, its

14

endeavors to discover truth, it does not know God. But the glory of God is to reveal himself, to show what he is like. The demonstration of what God is and does is the glory of God. Further help in understanding this is found in 2 Corinthians:

For it is the God who said, "Let light shine out of darkness," who has shone in our hearts to give the light of the knowledge of the glory of God in the face of Christ (2 Cor. 4:6).

Men can see the glory of God in the face of Christ, in his character, his being. And that glory is also found, says Paul, in "our hearts." The calling of the church is to reveal in the world the glory of God's character which is found in the face of Jesus Christ. This is stated again in chapter 1 of Ephesians:

He has put all things under his [Christ's] feet and has made him the head over all things for the church, which is his body, the fulness of him who fills all in all (Eph. 1:22,23).

That is a tremendous statement. It says that all that Jesus Christ is (his fullness) is to be seen in his body which is the church. The secret of the church is that Christ lives in it and the message of the church to the world is to declare him, to talk about Jesus Christ. Paul describes this secret of the true church again in the second chapter.

So then you are no longer strangers and sojourners, but you are fellow citizens with the saints and members of the household of God, built upon the foundation of the apostles and prophets, Christ Jesus himself being the chief cornerstone, in whom the whole structure is joined together and grows into a holy temple in the Lord; in whom you also are built into it for a dwelling place of God in the Spirit (Eph. 2:19-22).

15

There is the holy mystery of the church—it is the dwelling place of God. He lives in his people. That is the great calling of the church—to make visible the invisible Christ. Paul describes his own ministry as a pattern Christian in these terms:

> To make all men see what is the plan of the mystery hidden for ages in God who created all things; that through the church the manifold wisdom of God might now be made known to the principalities and powers in the heavenly places (Eph. 3:9, 10).

There it is very plainly. The task of the church is "to make known the manifold wisdom of God," make it known not only to men but also to angels who are observing the church. These are "the principalities and powers in the heavenly places." There are others besides men who are watching the church and learning from it.

Surely the verses above are enough to make one thing perfectly clear. The calling of the church is to declare in word and demonstrate in attitude and deed the character of Jesus Christ who lives within his people. We are to declare the reality of a life-changing encounter with a living Christ and to demonstrate that change by an unselfish, love-filled life. Until we have done that nothing else we can do will be of any avail. That is the calling of the church to which Paul refers when he said, *I beg you to lead a life worthy of the calling to which you have been called.*

Notice how the Lord Jesus himself confirms this in the opening chapter of the book of Acts. Just before Jesus ascended to his Father he said to his disciples:

> You shall receive power when the Holy Spirit has come upon you; and you shall be my witnesses in Jerusalem and in all Judea and Samaria and to the end of the earth (Acts 1:8).

The primary calling of the church is to be a witness

16

to Christ. A witness is one who declares and demonstrates. The apostle Peter has a wonderful word about this in his first letter:

You are a chosen race, a royal priesthood, a holy nation, God's own people, that you may declare the wonderful deeds of him who called you out of darkness into his marvelous light (I Peter 2:9).

Notice the structure, "<u>You are . . . that you may</u>." That is the primary task of the Christian. He is indwelt by Jesus Christ so that he may demonstrate the life and character of the one who lives within. The responsibility to fulfill this calling of the church belongs to every true Christian. All are called, all are indwelt by the Holy Spirit, all are expected to fulfill their calling in the midst of the world. That is the clear note the apostle sounds throughout the whole Ephesian letter. <u>The expression of the church's witness may sometimes be corporate, but the responsibility to do so is always individual</u>.

privilege = linked = responsibility

The True Marks of Jesus

But here the problem of a possible counterfeit emerges again. It is easy for the church (or the individual Christian) to talk about displaying the character of Christ and to make grandiose claims to be doing it. However, as every knowledgeable pagan knows who has observed Christians closely, <u>the image which actually comes through is not always the same as the Jesus of the Gospels</u>. That is why the apostle Paul is careful to describe that character in more specific terms.

. . . With all lowliness and meekness, with patience, forbearing one another in love, eager to maintain the unity of the Spirit in the bond of peace (Eph. 4:2,3).

<u>Humility, patience, love, unity and peace</u>—these are <u>the true marks of Jesus</u>. Christians are not to witness in arrogance and rudeness, not in holier-than-thou smug-

ness, not in sanctimonious presumption and certainly not against a background of ugly church fights and harshness between Christian and Christian. The church is not to talk about itself. It is to be lowly in mind, not proudly boasting of its power or seeking to advance its prestige. The church cannot save the world; but the Lord of the church can. It is not the church for which Christians are to labor and spend their lives, but for the Lord of that church. The church cannot exalt its Lord while it seeks to exalt itself. The true church does not seek to gain power in the eyes of the world. It already has all the power it needs from the Lord who indwells it.

Further, the church is to be patient and forbearing, knowing that the seeds of truth take time to sprout, grow and come to full harvest. The church is not to make strident demands upon society for sudden and tearing changes in long-established social patterns. Rather, the church is to resolutely refrain from the practice of social evils in its own midst and thus plant seeds of truth in a society which will ultimately win the day.

One of the famous books of all time is Edward Gibbon's *The Decline and Fall of the Roman Empire*.[2] He traces what happened to that mighty empire and how it disintegrated from within. In the book is a passage that Sir Winston Churchill memorized because he felt it so beautifully descriptive and accurate. It concerns the church within the empire.

"While that great body [the Roman empire] was invaded by open violence or undermined by slow decay, a pure and humble religion gently insinuated itself into the minds of men, grew up in silence and obscurity, derived new vigor from opposition, and finally erected

2. Edward Gibbon, *The Decline and Fall of the Roman Empire*, Vol. I (New York, The Modern Library), Random House, p. 382.

18

the triumphant banner of the Cross on the ruins of the Capitol."

The supreme mark of the life of Jesus Christ within the Christian is, of course, love. Love which accepts others as they are, is tenderhearted and forgiving, and seeks to prevent misunderstandings and differences of viewpoint from dividing Christians from each other. Jesus said, *By this all men will know that you are my disciples, if you have love for one another* (John 13:35). That love is never manifested by rivalry, greed, ostentatious display, indifference or prejudice. It is the very opposite of name-calling, backbiting, stubborn you-go-your-way-and-I'll-go-mine division. Love is concerned with maintaining unity, not creating it. The church can never create unity, only maintain it. We shall take a closer look at this theme in the next chapter.

But does not all this help us answer the great question, For what purpose is the church here in the world? Where shall we start in the task of influencing and changing the world? Where is our primary emphasis to be put? The New Testament has very little to say about Christian involvement in politics or substandard housing or civil rights or labor-capital squabbles. It is not that Christians should be unconcerned in these areas. Obviously you cannot have a heart filled with love for fellow human beings and not be concerned about these things. But the New Testament says relatively little about these things because God knows that the only way to help in these problems is to introduce a new dynamic into human life, the dynamic of the life of Jesus Christ. This is what men need. The correction of evil will inevitably follow the introduction of that life. Surely we must start there, for that is the calling to which the church is called.

Those who call themselves Christian radicals evidently do not understand the spiritual radicalism of the New Testament. The gospel germinated in a social milieu in many respects very similar to today's. The early Christians faced an establishment fighting for its life. There were widespread injustice, oppression, discrimination.

The Outside of the Cup

But those who look for proof texts to justify a picket line, a strike, a boycott or a lay-in are in trouble. These try to solve the ills of society by washing the outside of the cup, as Christ said. A true Christian revolution changes people from within. This is where churches so often go astray. Christ said, only as people are transformed, given a new heart, a new spirit and orientation, will there be a new society. There must be a dying to self and selfishness, a radical shift in direction, and a new birth or resurrection. The word of the Lord to such persons is, *Bless those who persecute you. . . . Live in harmony with one another. . . . Repay no one evil for evil. . . . Do not be overcome by evil, but overcome evil with good* (Rom. 12:14-21).

In this turbulent hour of history shall the church surrender the greatest revolutionary message the world has ever heard, a message specifically entrusted to the church? Instead, shall it content itself with doing what any worldly organization can do? Shall it become nothing more than another political action group? Shall it succumb to the fallacy that change, any kind of change, represents progress? What the apostle Paul desires is that we shall heed our calling to become individually responsible to tell this radical, revolutionary, life-transforming good news about Jesus Christ throughout society. The church must again invade commercial and industrial life, education and learning, the arts and family life, morals and government with this tremendous unequalled message. A risen Lord Jesus Christ is available to men everywhere to implant within them his own life and thus transform them into loving, concerned, confident people able to cope with whatever problems life may set before them. This is the calling of the church.

CHAPTER THREE

Not Union—Unity!

There is a certain set of voices in our day who say, "You are quite right about the need of the church to fulfill its calling. But fundamental to that calling is the union of all Christians. We can hardly expect to affect the world while Christians are so fragmented, so divided. In our disunity we really have nothing to say to the world and it is for this reason the church lives in weakness and is held in contempt by society. Therefore, above all other things our need is to unite. There is power in numbers and if we can get enough Christians together we can influence society as the church was intended to do."

This philosophy has given rise to the ecumenical movement of the latter part of the twentieth century.

Ecumenical means "universal" and it is the hope and dream of many in our day to dissolve the differences among Christians which the varying denominations represent and to bring about a truly ecumenical, or universal, church. Certain men have become so devoted to this ideal that they have been labelled "ecumaniacs," while others disdainfully suggest that the problem with the church is that it is passing through its "ecumenopause."

The words of the apostle Paul which we are examining do seem to lay stress upon the need for Christian unity. He exhorts the Ephesian Christians to be *eager to maintain the unity of the Spirit in the bond of peace* (Eph. 4:3). Other Scriptures underscore the need for Christian agreement. The ecumenicists say that when the churches unite in one organization it will be the fulfillment of the prayer of Jesus. *That they may all be one; as thou, Father, art in me, and I in thee, that they also may be one in us, so that the world may believe that thou hast sent me* (John 17:21). They say, "Why not welcome these modern efforts to produce that unity? Surely the union of all Christians can only strengthen and help the cause of Christ!"

A Glorious Mixture

What shall we make of this exhortation of Paul's to unity? One thing is clearly evident about it. It recognizes the existence of friction among Christians. He would not urge Christians to maintain the unity of the Spirit if there were not differences existing among them. Here in the early church there were obviously forces at work to divide the Christian body, there were pressures among them to break up into splinter groups. To counteract these pressures the apostle urges them to be eager to maintain unity. The word "eager" is a bit too weak, here. Eagerness implies mere willingness, but the original word in Greek meant willingness plus activity—actually doing something about it. The King James translation is more accurate, *earnestly endeavoring to keep the unity of the Spirit in the bond of peace*.

Certainly it is unrealistic for Christians to pretend there are no differences among them. There is no group in the world so gloriously heterogeneous as the church. Its genius is that it is made up of different kinds of people. In the true church of Christ the rich and poor are to gather on the same footing, without distinction and certainly without favor. Jews or Gentiles, men or women, black, red, white or yellow—it is to make no difference. This, admittedly, is not the way the church has always been, but this is the way the church was meant to be and can be. The church crosses all the boundaries which men erect and all natural distinctions as well, and gathers all peoples, without exception, into one body. No other body in the world attempts to unite people from such widely variant origins and backgrounds.

But we do not ignore these boundaries easily. Friction often arises because of them. That friction existed in the Christian communities of the first century is evident from several places in Scripture. There was the great divergence of viewpoint over the relation of the Gentiles to the Jews—a matter which necessitated the great council described in Acts 15. In Paul's letter to the Philippians two ladies are mentioned who had difficulty getting along with each other. Their names were Euodia and Syntyche (or, as they have been rendered, Odious and Soontouchy). Divergent viewpoints and personality differences are some of these same causes of friction existing in the church of the twentieth century as well.

> To dwell above with saints we love,
> Oh that will be glory.

24

But to live below, with saints we know;
Well, that's another story!

Besides differences of viewpoints and personalities
there are differences of gifts within the body of Christ.
Each Christian has a tendency to deprecate another's
gifts and to exalt his own. We all feel that what we are
contributing is much more important and valuable than
what others are doing. (First Corinthians 3 reveals the
division in the church of Corinth over the human
tendency to identify with one teacher as against another.) So there is fertile ground for friction arising
from differences and distinctions within the church.

But also in the apostle's exhortation a second fact is
visible. Beneath all the differences among the early
Christians there is also the fact of a basic unity. The
apostle does not tell these Christians to strive to produce unity, but to maintain what is already there. The
church is never told to create unity. There is a unity
that is already there by virtue of the very existence of
the church. There is no need to create it, in fact, men
are incapable of producing the unity that is essential to
the life of the church. It can be produced only by the
Spirit of God; but once produced, it is the responsibility of Christians to maintain it.

Three-in-One Unity

This is the trouble with the modern ecumenical
movement. Those who are striving to bring about the
union of Christians are ignoring the unity which already exists and are trying to produce another. To be
sure that no one misunderstands the nature of the unity
which the apostle refers to he goes on to describe it
clearly.

*There is one body, and one Spirit, just as you were
called to the one hope that belongs to your call, one
Lord, one faith, one baptism, one God and Father of us*

25

all, who is above all and through all and in all (Eph. 4:4-6).

Here is the true unity of the body of Christ. Notice that it gathers about the three Persons of the Trinity: Spirit, Son and Father. It is a body indwelt by the Triune God. That is clearly the answer to the prayer of Jesus: *that they may all be one; as thou, Father, art in me, and I in thee* (John 17:21). The church is not to be a conglomeration of individuals who happen to agree upon certain ideas. It is bound together as an organism in a bodily unity. It is true that a body is an organization but it is much more than an organization. The essence of a body is that it consists of thousands of cells with one mutually shared life.

Contrary to the old spiritual, a body is not produced by combining sections of anatomy together, by the toe bone being joined to the foot bone and the foot bone to the ankle bone and the ankle bone to the shin bone, etc. A body is formed by the extension of one original cell which grows until it becomes a mature body in which every cell shares the original life. That is the secret of the body—all parts of it share life together.

It is the sharing of life that makes a body different from an organization. An organization derives power from the association of individuals, but a body derives its power from the sharing of life. Dr. Bernard Ramm says:

"When modernists deny . . . a supernatural connectedness of all believers by the mystical union of the Holy Spirit, they destroy the historic, orthodox Christian understanding of the Church . . . The Church becomes a society, a natural, human, non-supernatural religious community. It is bound together by purely natural ties, such as a common heritage in the Bible, a common belief in some sort of uniqueness in Jesus, a common belief in the historical continuity of Christians, and a common ethic of love. Now the church is a society. But this is secondary to its being the supernatural body of Christ."[1]

Anyone who has had the privilege of contacting Christians in widespread places around the earth soon learns to recognize this fundamental unity which already exists. Despite denominational differences and widely varying degrees of theological viewpoint on many issues, wherever there is a mutual life in Christ it is immediately evident. There is a sense of belonging to each other. This unity is often discernible even when there is an official denial of it.

A number of years ago, I met with a Roman Catholic bishop in Mexico and spent an hour or two with him talking about Christ. I was a Protestant and he a Catholic, and if we had gone into doctrinal areas we would have found many differences of outlook. But with this particular bishop I sensed immediately a oneness which we shared together in Christ. He knew the reality of a living Lord, just as I did. We talked about him. Our organizations were not one, but we were one because we had entered into the experience of the unity of the Spirit.

The Power of the Church

That brings us to the next element in Paul's description of the unity of the church, one Spirit. This is the great, eternal, invisible Person who is the true power of the church. The strength of the church never derives from its numbers. The ecumenicists seek to create a unity of the flesh, an organizational unity which draws its power from the number of bodies which can be joined together, quite apart from conviction and spiritual agreement. Someone has well described such a

1. Bernard Ramm, *The Continental Divide in Contemporary Theology*, (Christianity Today, October, 8, 1965).

27

union as an attempt to put all corpses into one cemetery and thus to prepare for a resurrection. But it will
not work. The church is intended to be an instrument
of life, but putting dead bodies together does not produce life. The power of the church to influence society
does not derive from gathering together enough Christians to swing enough votes to sway a legislature.

The prophet Zechariah was once confronted with a
great mountain which God said would become a plain.
When Zechariah began to look around to see how this
would happen, where the power would come from to
level that mountain and make it into a plain, the word
of the Lord came to him, saying: *Not by might, nor by
power, but by my Spirit, saith the Lord of hosts* (Zech.
4:6). Impossible tasks require superhuman power.
Since the role of the church in the world is far
beyond the powers of men to fulfill, it is essential that
it rely on the only adequate power available. The Spirit
is the true power of the church. There is only one
Spirit. He is the same everywhere, no matter where the
church exists—in every place and in every age. The
Spirit does not change and that is why truth remains
unchangeable—the passing of time does not affect it.
That is also why the church is not dependent on many
or on few, or on the wisdom of its membership. It is to
depend on one thing, the Spirit of God. As we go on
into the apostle's words we shall learn more of how this
amazing power works.

Paul links with the Spirit, *the one hope that belongs
to your call* (Eph. 4:4). These first three factors of
unity are linked together (one body, one Spirit, one
hope) because it is the Spirit who forms the body for
its final and ultimate goal. What is that hope? It is expressed dozens of times throughout the Scriptures. It is
the hope of the return of Jesus Christ to earth and the
results this will have in the church and in the world.

Perhaps the briefest expression of it is found in Colossians, *Christ in you, the hope of glory* (Col. 1.27). Glory is the hope of the church. As John puts it . . . *we know that when he appears we shall be like him, for we shall see him as he is. And every one who thus hopes in him purifies himself as he is pure* (1 John 3:2,3).

Everywhere I have gone around the world I have found this to be the hope of Christians. No matter what their denomination, their background, their race or their color this is always the one hope: that they will someday be like Christ. There are many differences in understanding how this will work out. Some are premillenialists (believing that Christ will come before the millenium, a thousand-year reign of Christ on earth); others are postmillenialists (They say Christ returns after the millenium.) while others do not believe in a millenium at all. But there is only one final expectation of Christians everywhere and that is they will share the glory of Christ.

No Other Name

The apostle Paul next gathers up three more elements of unity around the second Person of the Trinity, the *one Lord*. He does not say, one Saviour, though it is true there is only one Saviour, but everywhere in Scripture it is only when men acknowledge Jesus as Lord that he becomes their Saviour. The fundamental issue which Paul centers on is that Jesus Christ is Lord. In writing to the Corinthians he says that no one can say "Jesus is Lord" except by the Holy Spirit.

"Lord" means ultimate authority. To call Jesus Lord is to recognize that he is the supreme person in the universe. There is no other Lord and there never will be another Lord. Peter puts it bluntly in Acts 4:12: *There is no other name under heaven, given among men, by*

29

which we must be saved. That is why the early Christians could not say "Caesar is Lord" as their persecutors sought to force them to say. That is why modern Christians cannot say, "Buddha is Lord" or that any other person is Lord but Jesus. The mystery and marvel of his person is that the man Christ Jesus, who lived and walked and loved and worked and died among men, whose life record is given to us in the Gospels, is also Lord of the universe, the Supreme Being, Lord of all things, the God-man. The apostle John, in his first letter, says that anyone who denies this is not a Christian but has the spirit of antichrist (1 John 2:22). And Paul declares, *Therefore God has highly exalted him and bestowed on him the name which is above every name, that at the name of Jesus every knee should bow, in heaven and on earth, and under the earth, and every tongue confess that Jesus Christ is Lord, to the glory of God the Father* (Phil. 2:9-11).

Linked to this is the next element, *one faith*. This is a little more difficult, but it seems clear that Paul does not refer to faith in general, i.e., the ability to believe, because all men have this. Sometimes men say. "I can't believe." But this is clearly untrue because men are believing all the time. All action comes from belief. An atheist acts from belief, just as does the Christian. They both believe something and act accordingly.

Nor does Paul mean the act of conversion when a person declares himself out and out for Christ—the initial step of believing and trusting in him—known as "saving faith." Paul is not speaking of these kinds of faith here. He has in view that which is believed, i.e., the body of truth which has been revealed. There is but one faith. It is what Jude refers to in his letter when he exhorts Christians, *Contend for the faith which was once for all delivered to the saints* (Jude 1:3).

This one faith is associated with Jesus the Lord. It is

the truth about him. Again, there may be differences on details and disagreement among Christians as to meaning, but there is everywhere full agreement among true Christians that there is but one body of truth about Jesus Christ. There is only one set of facts, one faith. That body of truth is the Scripture. There is not a faith for Jews and another set of facts for Gentiles; there is only one faith for all men everywhere. God has spoken through the seers, the prophets and the apostles, but it all forms one total picture, articulated and explaining itself. There is not, therefore, a God of the Old Testament versus a God of the New Testament, as we sometimes hear. Nor can we say, as some people do say, "Well, I have my Christ and you have yours." No, there is only one Christ. There is but one historic Jesus. There is but one faith.

The next element of unity is the *one baptism*. Unity about baptism? Nothing could seem farther from reality. All varieties of Baptists say, "This 'one baptism' is surely referring to water baptism, which is by immersion only." The Presbyterians say, "No, the Baptists are all wet, sprinkling is the only proper way." Other groups insist that baptism is for infants only while others say that it must be done only to consenting adults. There seems to be anything but unity on the question of baptism.

But despite this obvious difference over the symbol there is one baptism everywhere recognized and agreed upon by the church. It is the baptism of the Spirit, the real baptism, of which water baptism is the symbol. It is the means by which every true believer in Jesus Christ is made part of his living body, the church (1 Cor. 12:13). That baptism is here linked to Jesus Christ, the Lord, because it is baptism into his body. Romans 6:3 puts it this way, *we were all baptized into his death*. The central idea is that each individual believer is made to be one with Jesus Christ, united with him in all the value of his death and resurrection.

Our Father

The apostle now gives us the last of the seven elements of unity, *One God and Father of us all, who is above all and through all and in all* (Eph. 4:6). Here is the ultimate aim of the others. All the rest exist, as Peter puts it, to *bring us to God* (1 Pet. 3:18). He is the goal and the aim.

The sign that we have found him is that we recognize him as Father, we sense his father-heart. You know how Paul puts it in Romans 8: *You have received the spirit of sonship when we cry, "Abba! Father!"* (Rom. 8:15). John writes in his first letter that the unmistakable mark of a new-born babe in the family of God is that he immediately knows his father, and calls him Father. (1 John 2:13)

What a far cry this is from some of the views of God which are abroad today. He is called The Ground of Being, The Ultimate Cause, The Infinite Mind, etc. It is true that God is all these things. They are not wrong but they are very inadequate. Paul, too, agrees that God is *above all and through all and in all* (Eph. 4:6). He is the end and the beginning; he is the beginning and the end. All things exist because of him and all things are trending toward him. Beautiful language here, and all true! But when you actually know him you find he can only be properly addressed as Father. No other name will express the intimate union with God which a true Christian feels. That is why Jesus taught his disciples to say, "Our Father, you who are in heaven."

In these seven elements is found the nature of Christian unity. Not a union to be produced, but a unity which already exists. They are not, therefore, articles of theological agreement. They ought never to be put into a creedal statement as though agreement with these is what makes someone become a Christian. No, it is rather that becoming a Christian brings agreement on these points. They are areas of mutual experience. They are experienced truth which lays hold of us, not truths which we are to lay hold of. They are not debatable. If anyone challenges or disagrees with these he is simply manifesting the fact that he is not yet a Christian. When he becomes a Christian he will experience and therefore understand these things. He may not be able to articulate them clearly but he will recognize them when they are described, for they are immediately experienced by all who are in Christ. Therefore, the way to create unity is simply to bring men and women to Christ and the unity of the Spirit will be produced in them by the Spirit. It is impossible to achieve any meaningful or significant union apart from this unity which is produced only by the Spirit.

Putting it in another way, there are two kinds of unity: an external unity without internal agreement, and internal unity which manifests occasional external disagreement. We have been calling the first, union. By the very nature of the case, control and direction in this kind of a group always rests with a small number at the top. Their power is measured by how successful they are in getting the conglomerate to follow them.

I remember well the first time I ran into the second kind of unity, the internal. As a boy I had two friends who were brothers, only a year apart in age. One day we were out playing (messing around, as kids say today) and these brothers fell to quarrelling. I thought that one was a bit sarcastic and unfair so I chimed in on behalf of the underdog. To my amazement he did not welcome my help but turned on me, and his brother joined him and both jumped on me. I discovered I had made a very shallow judgment. I felt the differences they were airing represented a fundamental disagreement between them but not at all! Underneath there was a fundamental unity, and the moment I attacked one of them it manifested itself and they both turned on me. This illustrates the unity of the church: an internal unity with occasional external disagreement.

Now there are certain practical conclusions which come from a passage like Ephesians 4:4-6. As we apply this great central truth of Christian unity to the outer areas of our lives, especially as we confront the problems of modern existence, there are certain things that become immediately evident. First, it is clear that Christians are to direct their efforts not at producing an outward union but toward maintaining peace within the body. That is clearly what Paul says: *eager to maintain the unity of the Spirit in the bond of peace* (Eph. 4:3). It is extremely important that Christians stop quarreling, bickering, struggling against one another, and feeling strong resentment and hate. A church where these attitudes exist is a totally ineffective body in its community. Such a church can say nothing to which the world will pay any attention.

Called to Understand

It is important that when Christians meet together they recognize that they are called to understand one another. They are to forbear one another, to pray for one another, to forgive one another, to be kind, tenderhearted, not holding grudges, not being bitter, resentful, or hateful toward each other. This is where the Spirit aims when he comes into our midst. He moves toward the healing of long-standing grudges, deepseated resentments, and bitter hostilities.

Christians must do what the apostle says: maintain the unity of the Spirit. The unity is already there, it

34

simply needs to be made evident. We must get below the surface, behind the differences that are all too apparent, and then the fundamental unity will be evident. If there has been work of grace at all, the marvelous, underlying, fundamental unity that is there will come welling up past all the differences and express itself, by the Spirit of Jesus Christ, in love manifested even to the unlovely.

A second conclusion from this passage is that we cannot classify Christians by organizations. We cannot say that all Catholics are Christians or that all Baptists are. We cannot maintain that all who belong to the Independent Fundamental Churches of America are Christians while all those who belong to the World Council of Churches are not. God's Spirit forever overleaps human boundaries. The unity of the Spirit will be found in people in many different groups and we must recognize that fact. We shall find true Christians everywhere and it becomes our responsibility to maintain the unity of the Spirit in the bond of peace with them wherever we find them. As Paul says in Romans 14, *As for the man who is weak in faith, welcome him, but not for disputes over opinions* (Rom. 14:1). We are not to cast him out but to receive him. Receive him even though he does not see as clearly as you do and perhaps has not graduated from the right school. Nevertheless, receive him. Recognize him as a brother if he manifests love for Jesus Christ, no matter what his label may be.

A third practical conclusion from this study is that true Christians may use the fact of basic internal unity to determine the area and kind of cooperation they can have with others, both Christian and non-Christian. After all, though we may not be one with everyone else as members of the body of Christ, we are one in sharing human life. We can join with anyone in the relief

35

of human ailments, in establishing strong and just government, in pursuit of education, and in many other enterprises in life. We are not to shut ourselves away from other human beings because they do not share the same life in Christ.

Opposite Direction

But there is also an area where we can cooperate with some Christians who share the life of Jesus Christ, but cannot join with others. That area is in the enterprise of proclaiming the great life-changing message of the church, in evangelizing the world. The reason for this is that many who regard themselves as Christians have an understanding of the gospel that is entirely different from ours. What they are attempting to do among men is entirely different than what we seek. We and they go in two opposite directions. It is impossible, of course, to ride two horses going in opposite directions—to attempt it is to put a terrific strain upon the anatomy. The Israelites of old were taught this same truth when they were told not to yoke an ox and an ass together. (Deut. 22:10) Why not? Because they go at two different speeds and are two different heights. They would simply chafe one another all the time. It would be cruelty to link them together. This is God's way of teaching symbolically that there are fundamental differences of gait and direction between people and that two cannot walk together except they be agreed. (Amos 3:3)

But someone may ask: "Can we worship together with others who do not share life in Jesus Christ?" The answer of the Bible is clearly, yes. God commands all men everywhere to worship him (Ps. 65:2; Phil. 2:10, 11). Wherever anyone is worshiping God as supreme and not some lesser concept of him (as an idol) then Christians can join together with such in worship. The

36

most elementary path for the approach of anyone to God is declared in Hebrews 11:6: . . . *whoever would draw near to God must believe that he exists and that he rewards those who seek him.* Cornelius, the Roman centurion, described in Acts 10, is an example of just such a person.

Having said all this, let us not forget the appeal of the apostle to the church to be faithful to its calling. The church does not have the right to chart its own course. Its purpose and goal has already been set, and even its function has been determined by its Lord. In the next section of Ephesians 4 the apostle turns to a detailed description of the equipment provided by the Lord for his body to function as he intends it should in the world.

CHAPTER FOUR

All God's Children Have Gifts

God's program for reaching and changing a broken world has always been one involving incarnation. When God chose to visit this earth to demonstrate to mankind the new kind of life he was offering, he did so by incarnating himself. God became flesh and dwelt among us. Jesus Christ was that incarnation of God— God in human flesh appearing among men. But that was only the beginning of the process of incarnation. We shall make a great mistake if we think incarnation ended with the earthly life of Jesus. The incarnation is still going on. The life of Jesus is still being manifest among men, but now no longer through an individual physical body, limited to one place on earth, but through a complex, corporate body called the church.

Open the book of Acts in the New Testament and

you will find that Dr. Luke, the writer, tells a certain young man named Theophilus that he had set down in his first account (the Gospel According to Luke) "all that Jesus *began* to do and teach." In his second account (the book of Acts) Dr. Luke continues the record of Jesus at work among mankind, but this time through his new body, the church. The church, therefore, when it lives in and by the Spirit, is to be nothing more nor less than the extension of the life of Jesus to the whole world in any age.

That is an all-important concept. What happened on a small scale in Judea and Galilee nineteen hundred years ago is intended to happen on a large scale throughout the whole world today, permeating every level of society and every aspect of human life. As Christians discover this to be a live possibility today their lives become exciting and powerfully effective. It is challenging and stimulating to rediscover the pattern by which God has designed that his church should influence the world. On the other hand, there is nothing more pathetic and abortive than a church which does not understand this fascinating program for the operating of the body of Christ and substitutes instead business methods, organizational procedures, and pressure politics as means to influence society.

Let us then look at this exciting pattern of operation which the apostle Paul describes as the way by which the body of Jesus Christ touches and changes the world. Paul now turns from his description of the nature of the church to the provision made by the Holy Spirit for its operation. He says, *But grace was given to each of us according to the measure of Christ's gift* (Eph. 4:7).

A New Capacity for Service

In that brief sentence there is a reference to two tremendous things: the gift of the Holy Spirit for ministry given to every true Christian without exception, and the new and remarkable power by which that gift may be exercised. We must look carefully at both of these in due order, but let us begin with the gift of the Spirit which Paul calls here a "grace."

The word in the original language is *charis* from which the English adjective, charismatic, is derived. This "grace" is a capacity for service which is given to every true Christian without exception and which was something each did not possess before he became a Christian. Paul himself, in chapter 3, verse 8 of this same letter refers to one of the gifts which he possessed: *To me, though I am the very least of all the saints, this grace (charis) was given.* What was the grace? He goes on: *To preach to the Gentiles the unsearchable riches of Christ.* Clearly one of his gifts was that of preaching, or as it is called in other places, the gift of prophesying. When Paul writes to his young son in the faith, Timothy, he uses a closely related word and says to him, *Hence I remind you to rekindle the gift (charisma) of God that is within you* (2 Tim. 1:6).

There seems little doubt that this is where the early church began with new converts. Whenever anyone, by faith in Jesus Christ, passed from the kingdom and power of Satan into the kingdom of God's love, he was immediately taught that the Holy Spirit of God had not only imparted to him the life of Jesus Christ, but had also equipped him with a spiritual gift or gifts which he was then responsible to discover and exercise. The apostle Peter writes to certain Christians (1 Pet. 4:10) and says, *As each has received a gift, employ it for one another, as good stewards of God's varied grace.* Again, in 1 Corinthians 12:7 Paul writes: *To each is given the manifestation of the Spirit for the common good.* It is very significant that in each place where the gifts of

40

the Spirit are described in Scripture the emphasis is placed upon the fact that each Christian has at least one. That gift may be lying dormant, inchoate, unused. You may not know what it is, but it is there; for the Holy Spirit makes no exceptions to this basic equipping of each believer. It is vitally essential that you discover the gift or gifts which you possess, for the value of your life as a Christian will be determined by the degree to which you use that which God has provided you.

The most detailed passage on the gifts of the Spirit is 1 Corinthians 12. There is another briefer list in Romans 12, and a still shorter list in 1 Peter 4. In these passages certain gifts are referred to by more than one name. In comparing the passages it seems evident that there are sixteen or seventeen basic gifts and these may be found in various combinations within a single individual, each cluster of gifts opening the door to a wide and varied ministry.

Perhaps the most helpful way to become acquainted with these gifts is to allow the apostle Paul to teach us concerning them from the great explanation he gives to the church at Corinth:

Now there are varieties of gifts, but the same Spirit; and there are varieties of service, but the same Lord; and there are varieties of working, but it is the same God who inspires them all in every one (1 Cor. 12:4-6).

Notice the three divisions of the subject of spiritual gifts. There are gifts; there are ministries (called "service" here); and there are workings (or energizings). Gifts are linked to the Spirit, ministries are linked to the Lord Jesus, and workings are linked to God, the Father. Thus, as in Ephesians 4, the triune God is seen dwelling within his body, the church, for the specific purpose of ministering to a broken world (Eph. 4:3-6).

A gift, as we have already noted, is a specific capacity or function. A ministry is the sphere in which a gift is performed, among a certain group of people, or in a certain geographic area. It is the prerogative of the Lord Jesus to assign a sphere of service for each member of his body. You can see him exercising that right in the twenty-first chapter of the Gospel of John. There, after his resurrection, he appears to Peter and three times bids him, "Feed my sheep." That was to be Peter's ministry. He was to be a pastor (or elder), feeding the flock of God. (Peter refers to himself in this capacity in the fifth chapter of his first letter.) When Peter expresses curiosity as to what the Lord would have John do, the Lord says to him, *What is that to you? Follow me!* (see John 21:15-23.) The Lord is still exercising this right today. He sets some to the task of teaching Christians, others he sends to minister to the worldly. To some he gives the task of training youth and to others a ministry to older people. Some work with women and others with men; some go to the Jews, others to the Gentiles. Peter was sent to the circumcised (the Jews), while Paul was sent to the uncircumcised (the Gentiles). They both had the same gift but their ministry was different.

Then there are workings, or energizings. These are the responsibility of the Father. The term refers to the degree of power by which a gift is manifested or ministered on a specific occasion. *There are varieties of working*, the apostle says, *but it is the same God who inspires them all in every one* (1 Cor. 12:6). Every exercise of a spiritual gift does not produce the same result each time. The same message given in several different circumstances will not produce the same results. What is the difference? It is God's choice. He does not intend to produce the same results every time. He could, but he does not always desire to do so. It is up to the Father to determine how much is accomplished at each ministry of a gift. The Scriptures record that

John the Baptist did no miracle throughout the course of his ministry. Yet he was a mighty prophet of God and Jesus said of him that there is no man born of woman who is greater than he (see Matt. 11:11). There are those today who suggest that if we cannot do miracles it is a sign of weakness in faith and of low spiritual power. But John did no miracles. Why not? Because there are varieties of workings, and it was not the choice of the Father to work through John in that way.

Now, in 1 Corinthians 12, we come to the list of specific spiritual gifts.

Twin Gifts

To one is given through the Spirit the utterance of wisdom, and to another the utterance of knowledge according to the same Spirit . . . (v. 8).

Here is a pair of gifts: the gifts of wisdom and knowledge. These often appear together in a single individual, for they are related to the same function. They are concerned with utterance, or as it is in the original, the word. The gift of knowledge is the ability to perceive and systematize the great facts which God has hidden in his word. A person exercising this gift is able to recognize the key and important facts of Scripture as a result of investigation. The gift of wisdom, on the other hand, is the ability to apply those insights to a specific situation. It is wisdom which is capable of putting knowledge to work. Perhaps you have been in a meeting where some problem was being discussed and there is a seeming impasse—no one seems to know what to do or what the answer is. Then someone will stand up and take some great principle of Scripture and apply it to the problem in such a clear way that everyone can see the answer. That is the gift of wisdom being exercised.

These twin gifts of wisdom and knowledge are also

related to the gift of teaching which is mentioned at the end of chapter 12. Teaching deals with communication. It is the ability to impart the facts and insights which the gifts of knowledge and wisdom discover; to pass them on to others in learnable form. The man or woman who possesses all three of these gifts is a valuable person to have around, indeed.

Then Paul mentions the gift of faith. This faith is again different from what we discussed in chapter 3. What Paul means here is essentially what we call today the gift of vision. It is the ability to see something that needs to be done and to believe that God will do it even though it looks impossible. Trusting that sense of faith, a person with this gift moves out and accomplishes the thing in God's name. Every great Christian enterprise has been begun by a man or woman who possessed the gift of faith. Some years ago, in the island of Taiwan, I met a remarkable woman named Mrs. Lillian Dickson. Clearly and unmistakably she has the gift of faith. When she sees a need she moves right in to meet it, regardless of whether she can see an adequate supply of funds or resources. She became concerned about certain poor boys on the streets of Taipei who have no homes. They are orphans or have been cast adrift by their families. Her heart went out to them because of the pressures that force them into a life of crime. Because she has the gift of faith she did something about them. She started an organization to rescue those boys, and all over the world people send her money for that and other projects which she supervises. That is the gift of faith in action.

Healing at Every Level

Then the apostle mentions "gifts of healing" given by the same Spirit. The word in the original Greek is in the plural, "healings." I take that to mean healing at every level of human need: bodily, emotionally, and spiritually.

In the early church there were a number of instances where this gift was exercised on the physical level. Throughout church history there have been others who had this gift of physical healing. There are some today who call themselves "healers," but it is of interest that none of the apostles ever made this claim for themselves. However, there is abundant evidence in the New Testament that the Spirit of God worked through the apostles and other believers in bringing physical healing to the sick, just as he does today. Some claims to healing today are based on spectacular temporary improvement as a result of strong psychological conditioning, and the healing fades away within a few days. But that God does heal today, sometimes quickly and permanently, is too well attested to challenge. We only note here that such healing does not necessarily indicate that the gift of healing is being exercised.

If someone asks, "Why is this gift so infrequently bestowed today?" the answer is given in verse 11 of 1 Corinthians 12: *All these are inspired by one and the same Spirit who apportions to each one individually as he wills.* The spiritual gift of physical healing is not seen often today because it is not the will of the Spirit for it to be given in these days as widely as it was in the early church.

The gift of healing is, however, frequently bestowed today on the emotional and spiritual level. Many Christians, laymen and professional ministers alike, are equipped by the Spirit to help those with damaged emotions and with bruised spirits, who have become sick or deranged in these areas. They make excellent counsellors because they are able to exercise the patience and compassion necessary to help such wounded souls.

45

Along this same line is the gift of miracles. This is the ability to short-circuit the processes of nature by supernatural activity, as the Lord did when he turned water into wine or multiplied the loaves and fishes. Some may still have this gift today. I don't doubt that it can be given; but again, I have never met anyone who had the gift of miracles, though perhaps some have exercised this at times in the history of the church.

The gifts of physical healing, miracles and tongues are given for the initial building up of faith, as a bridge to move Christians on from dependence upon things they can see to faith in a God who can work and accomplish much when nothing seems to be happening. The history of missions will substantiate this. God wants us to walk by faith, not by sight.

The apostle goes on to mention the gift of prophecy. This is the greatest gift of all as Paul makes clear by devoting an entire chapter (1 Corinthians 14) to the praise of this gift. We shall examine the gift of prophecy more fully when we return to Ephesians 4 and the ministry of the prophet. But here in verse 3 of 1 Corinthians 14 the apostle says of this gift, *On the other hand, he who prophesies speaks to men for their upbuilding and encouragement and consolation.* That is the effect of the gift of prophecy. When a man or woman has this gift it results in building, stimulating, and encouraging others. This is not a gift for preachers only. All the gifts are given without respect to a person's training. Many laymen and laywomen have the gift of prophecy and should be exercising it.

Then there is the gift of discernment of spirits. This is the ability to distinguish between the spirit of error and the spirit of truth before the difference is manifest to all by the results. It is the ability to see through a phony before his phoniness is clearly evident. When

46

Ananias and Sapphira came to Peter, bringing what they claimed to be the full price of some land they had sold though they had actually kept back part of it for themselves, Peter exercised the gift of discernment when he said, *How is it that you have agreed together to tempt the Spirit of the Lord? You have not lied to men but to God* (Acts 5:4,9). Those who have this gift can read a book and sense the subtlety of error in it, or hear a message and put their finger on what may be wrong about it. It is a valuable gift to have exercised within the church.

Another pair of gifts is listed next: tongues and interpretation of tongues. Recently there has been a renewal of interest in these gifts, especially in the Roman Catholic and other liturgical churches. All such movements must be examined in the light of the Scriptures. Do they glorify Christ? Is there ample biblical authority for their teachings? Do they promote unity in the body of Christ? Are their followers characterized by Christ-like holiness, humility and love? Do they bring permanent improvement to the individual and to the church?

Distinctive Marks

The biblical gift of tongues had at least three distinctive marks which are clearly described in the New Testament. First, as on the day of Pentecost, the gift of tongues consisted of known languages spoken somewhere on earth. The description "unknown tongue" which appears in the *King James Version* has no support in the original Greek text. The tongues of the New Testament were not a torrent of unrelated syllables, but had structure and syntax, as any earthly language has.

Second, the biblical gift was praise and thanksgiving addressed to God. Paul wrote, *For one who*

speaks in a tongue speaks not to men but to God
(1 Cor. 14:2). The gift of tongues is definitely not a
means of preaching the gospel or of conveying messages
to groups or individuals; but is, as it was on the day of
Pentecost, a means of praising God for his mighty works.

Third, the gift of tongues was intended as a sign to
unbelievers and not as a sign for believers. Paul is very
precise about this. He quotes the prophet Isaiah as
having predicted the purpose of tongues: *In the law it
is written, "By men of strange tongues and by the lips
of foreigners will I speak to this people, and even then
they will not listen to me, says the Lord." Thus,
tongues are a sign not for believers but for unbelievers,
while phophecy is not for unbelievers but for believers*
(1 Cor. 14:21,22). The appearance of this gift marked
the fact that God was judging the nation Israel and
turning from it to the Gentiles. This is why Peter said
to the Jews on the day of Pentecost, *For the promise
is to you and to your children [Jews] and to all that
are far off [Gentiles], every one whom the Lord our God
calls to him* (Acts 2:39).

Although it is not explicitly stated in Scripture as
a distinguishing characteristic of the biblical gift of
tongues, nevertheless, it is a striking fact that the gift
was everywhere publicly exercised and was evidently
not intended for private use. We are told that the gifts
of the Spirit are for the common good, and not for
personal benefit. Each occasion with which tongues is
connected in the New Testament was a public meeting. The setting for 1 Corinthians 14 is the assembly
of Christians together for mutual ministry and worship. When a Christian exercised the gift in prayer and
thanksgiving to God it was valueless to the church
unless it was interpreted, though the one exercising it
received certain edification in his own spirit.

Paul forbids its exercise in church unless there was definite assurance of interpretation for the edification of those present.

Since the gift of tongues is the easiest of the gifts to imitate, there have been imitations of it through the centuries. Whether those manifestations are the true gift or not can only be determined by their agreement with the biblical marks. Let us remember that the primary purpose of any gift of the Spirit is to minister to the body of Christ for its edification and strengthening, and to accomplish the specific aim of the Holy Spirit in giving the gift.

At the close of 1 Corinthians 12 there is another list of the spiritual gifts, some of which duplicate the gifts already discussed:

And God has appointed in the church first apostles, second prophets, third teachers, then workers of miracles, then healers, helpers, administrators, speakers in various kinds of tongues (v. 28).

We shall reserve the consideration of apostles, prophets and teachers till a later chapter, for these belong to a special class of gifts. The gifts of miracles and of healings we have already looked at, but a wonderful gift is mentioned here for the first time. It is the gift of helps. In some ways this is one of the greatest gifts and certainly it is the most widespread. It is the ability to lend a hand wherever a need appears, but to do it in such a way that it strengthens and encourages others spiritually. In the church it is often manifest in those who serve as ushers and treasurers, in those who prepare the Communion table or arrange flowers and serve dinners. More than most people realize, the exercise of this gift makes possible the ministry of the other, more evident, gifts. Every church is deeply indebted to those who exercise the gift of helps.

In the twelfth chapter of Romans is another partial

treatment of spiritual gifts, in verses 6-8: *Having gifts that differ according to the grace given to us, let us use them: if prophecy, in proportion to our faith; if service, in our serving; he who teaches, in his teaching; he who exhorts, in his exhortation; he who contributes, in liberality; he who gives aid, with zeal; he who does acts of mercy, with cheerfulness.*

We have already touched briefly upon the gift of prophecy and shall study it further when we return to Ephesians 4. The gift of serving seems to be identical with the gift of helps just examined. The word for serving is the same Greek word from which the word "deacon" comes. A deacon then would be anyone who uses his gift of helps to perform a service on behalf of or in the name of the church.

Exhorting, Giving, Leading

The gift of teaching we have already considered as having to do with the realm of communication of truth. The next gift in this list is that of exhortation. This is a word which means to encourage or comfort another. Its Greek root means "to call alongside" and gives us the picture of someone calling another to come alongside for strengthening or reassurance. It is the same root from which a name of the Holy Spirit is derived: the Comforter, or in the *RSV*, the Counselor. Those who have this gift are able to inspire others to action, awaken renewed spiritual interest, or steady those who are buffeted or faltering.

Another gift mentioned for the first time here is that of contributing, or of giving. It is fundamentally money that is in view and therefore the exhortation is to give with liberality. It may surprise many to learn that the Holy Spirit gives such a gift as this, but many Christians possess it, both the wealthy and the poor. It is the ability to earn and give money for the advancement

50

of God's work and to do so with such wisdom and cheerfulness that the recipients are immeasurably strengthened and blessed by the transaction. I have had men with the gift of giving come to me and offer to finance a ministry at considerable cost to themselves. They derive obvious joy and satisfaction from the results obtained.

The next gift listed is widely misunderstood because it is poorly translated. The *RSV* says that he who "gives aid" is to do it with zeal. *Phillips* is closer: *Let the man who wields authority think of his responsibility;* and the *New English Bible* is right on, with: *If you are a leader, exert yourself to lead.* This might best be called the gift of leadership. The Greek word is literally, "one who stands in front." It is clearly evidenced in emceeing meetings, conducting panels, chairing organizations, etc., but especially to do so in a way which helps others spiritually.

The final gift mentioned in Romans 12 is that of doing acts of mercy. Its distinctiveness is indicated by the word "mercy." Mercy is undeserved aid, aid given to those who often revolt others—the deformed, the smelly, the unpleasing. It differs from the gift of helps by being directed to the undeserving, regardless of their condition. I know a young woman who has this gift and has developed a remarkable ministry of aid and comfort to retarded children. The love and patience she shows toward them is beautiful to watch.

Here, then, are the "graces" which are distributed by the Holy Spirit to each member of the body of Christ as the Spirit chooses. There are no exceptions to this, there is no one left out. This is the fundamental provision of the Lord for the operation of his church. As a physical human body consists of numerous cells exercising various functions, so the body of Christ consists of many members, each of whom possesses a specific function that is absolutely essential to the proper operation of the body.

It is obvious that there can be no hope of ever getting the church to operate as it was intended to do until each individual member recognizes and begins to exercise the spiritual gift or gifts which he has received. So fundamentally important is this that we shall take an extra chapter to look at the gifts from a wider point of view and give practical help on how to recognize them in yourself, and how to put them to work.

CHAPTER FIVE

Understanding Your Gift

The church is primarily and fundamentally a body designed to express through each individual member the life of an indwelling Lord and is equipped by the Holy Spirit with gifts designed to express that life. To become aware that God himself has equipped you— yes, YOU—with a uniquely designed pattern of spiritual gifts and has placed you exactly where he wants you in order to minister those gifts, is to enter a whole new dimension of exciting possibility. In all the world there is no experience more satisfying and fulfilling than to realize that you have been the instrument of the divine working in the lives of others. Such an experience awaits any true Christian who is willing to give time and thought to the discovery and understanding of his

53

pattern of gifts, and will submit himself to the authority of the Head of the body, who reserves to himself the right to coordinate and direct its activities.

The Deepest Level

One of the important facts to get clearly in mind in an attempt to understand spiritual gifts is to realize that a spiritual gift is not the same as a natural talent. It is true that talents such as musical ability, artistic skills, athletic coordination, etc., are also gifts from God. But they are gifts on a physical or social level only, given to benefit mankind in its "natural" life. Spiritual gifts, on the other hand, are given for benefit in the realm of the spirit, the realm of an individual's relationship to God. The effect of the operation of a spiritual gift is to improve a person in his spirit's enjoyment of the life and love of God—to bless him, in other words. Moreover, since the spirit is the most fundamental part of man's being, from which all other relationships flow, it is clear that the exercise of spiritual gifts operates at the deepest level of human existence, and strikes right at the root of all human problems. Talents, however, deal more with the surfaces of life and though useful or entertaining, do not permanently change men as spiritual gifts can do.

Talents, obviously, are distributed to men and women quite apart from any reference to their spiritual condition. Non-Christians, as well as Christians, have talents and both can find many opportunities for useful expression of their talents in both religious and secular ways. But only Christians have spiritual gifts, for they are given only to those in whom the Spirit of Christ has come to dwell (1 Cor. 12:7).

It is quite possible, therefore, for a Christian to have a talent for teaching, for instance, but not to have the spiritual gift of teaching. If that is the case and he were asked to teach a Sunday School class, as an example, he would be quite capable of imparting considerable information and knowledge of facts about the lessons to his class but his teaching would lack the power to bless, to advance his students spiritually. This fact helps to explain the many qualified secular teachers who do not do well at all as Sunday School teachers. On the other hand, many school teachers also possess, as Christians, the spiritual gift of teaching and are greatly used of God in Bible classes and Sunday School teaching.

It is also quite possible to exercise a spiritual gift through the channel of a natural talent. This is frequently seen in the ministry of Christian singers. We have all heard Christian soloists with great voices whose evident musical talents would have pleased secular audiences anywhere. But in addition they possessed great power to impart spiritual enrichment through their singing, leaving their audiences spiritually refreshed and strengthened. Most often it is the gift of exhortation that the singer is exercising, but it is being carried by his musical talent as man is carried by a horse. Of course we have all been treated also to the painful experience of listening to a Christian sing without exercising any spiritual gift and finding our hearts left cold and unmoved by a performance of technical excellence but without spiritual power. The lesson is clear: don't try to use your natural talents to accomplish the work of God, for talents cannot operate in that sphere. But do use them as channels or vehicles for spiritual gifts and you will find they dovetail beautifully just as you might expect they would since they both come from the same God.

Perhaps the question most pressing upon you right now is: how do I discover my spiritual gifts? If they are the doorway to a new world of fulfillment and challenge then I surely want to know what mine are, but just how do I go about it? The answer is really very simple. <u>You discover a spiritual gift just like you discovered your natural talents</u>!

A Special Appeal

How did you find out that you were musically talented? Or artistically endowed? Or able to lead, to organize, to run, or to paint? <u>Probably it began first with some kind of desire. You simply *liked* whatever it is you are talented at, and found yourself drawn toward those who were already doing it.</u> You enjoyed watching those who were good at it, and came to appreciate something of the fine points of the activity. That is the way spiritual gifts make themselves known at first too. Somewhere the idea has found deep entrenchment in Christian circles that doing what God wants you to do is always unpleasant; that Christians must always make choices between doing what they want to do and being happy, and doing what God wants them to do and being completely miserable.

Nothing could be more removed from truth. <u>The exercise of a spiritual gift is always a satisfying, enjoyable experience though sometimes the occasion on which it is exercised may be an unhappy one.</u> Jesus said it was his constant delight to do the will of the one who sent him. The Father's gift awakened his own desire and he went about doing what he intensely enjoyed doing. So, <u>as a Christian, start with the gifts you most feel drawn toward. Study the biblical lists of gifts and try those which make special appeal to you.</u>

<u>Then, the next step is to watch for improvement and development.</u> Do you get better at it as you go along? Do you find your quite understandable initial fears subsiding and a growing competence developing? Remember, that's the way it was in discovering your tal-

ents, too. Gifts need to be exercised just as talents do and practice tends to make more perfect in one just as much as in the other. Paul wrote to young Timothy, telling him, *Rekindle the gift of God that is within you* (2 Tim. 1:6). As skill in the exercise of a gift develops, the spiritual blessing it brings will become increasingly evident. You will find yourself more and more seeking occasions in which you may manifest your gift, but never, of course, for your own personal advancement but always for the enrichment and profit of others. As Paul reminds us: *to each is given the manifestation of the Spirit for the common good* (1 Cor. 12:7).

Do you have a certain spiritual gift, or don't you? A final test is this: Do others recognize this gift in you? When someone says to you, quite unsolicited, "We'd like you to take on this ministry, we think you have a gift for it," then you can be quite sure that you have that spiritual gift. It may well be that others will see it long before you do. In fact one of the most helpful ways the members of Christ's body can minister to each other is to help one another discover spiritual gifts. It is much better for others to tell you what gifts they see in you than for you to lay pretentious claims to gifts you might not actually have. One great Bible teacher used to say it was a great pity to see someone who thought he had the gift of preaching, but no one had the gift of listening!

It is helpful, also, to realize that hardly anyone discovers all his gifts at the beginning of his Christian experience. Gifts, like talents, may lie undiscovered for years and then a certain combination of circumstances may bring them to light. It is wise, therefore, to be always ready to try something new. Who knows but what the Spirit of God has put you on the doorstep of a new endeavor for the express purpose of helping you discover gifts you never knew you had.

Is it proper to pray for a certain specific gift to be given you? Bible teachers differ on the answers to this one. Some feel that the pattern of gifts you may possess are all determined by the Spirit at the moment he takes up his residence within you. It may take you years to discover your gifts, but they were all there at the beginning and no new ones are ever added. Others point to the verse, *But earnestly desire the higher gifts* (1 Cor. 12:31), and feel that this encourages prayer for specific gifts. It should be noted that this exhortation is in the plural and is closer to a Southern "you all" (or "y'all") than to the individual "you." It would then mean that the apostle wanted these Corinthian believers to pray that God would manifest the best gifts in their midst by sending among them individuals equipped with these gifts, but it was not meant for individual encouragement to seek specific gifts. However, in 1 Corinthians 14:13 Paul does say, *He who speaks in a tongue should pray for the power to interpret*. Whatever else is meant by these verses, it is clear that certain gifts are more useful and profitable than others, and every church is to be concerned that the best ones are in evidence in their midst. Certainly the final choice is left up to the Spirit, for Paul says that he *apportions to each one individually as he wills* (1 Cor. 12:11). Hebrews 2:4 also speaks of *gifts of the Holy Spirit distributed according to his own will*.

Infinite Variety

In the preceding chapter we mentioned the fact that the gifts, though only about 17 or 18 in number, are given in clusters or combinations which make possible an almost infinite number of varying ministries. Judging from the analogy of the natural world it is highly likely that no two Christians have exactly the same pattern of gifts. Therefore no two have exactly the same ministry. No two faces in the world are precisely alike yet all are made up from the same basic features: two eyes, two ears, one nose, one mouth, two cheeks, one chin and one forehead. God gave you your face because it is exactly right for the expression of his life where you are. Likewise he gives you the precise cluster of gifts you possess because it is just what is needed for the ministry the Lord Jesus will indicate for you.

Do you see what this means? It completely eliminates all competition within the body of Christ! No Christian needs to be the rival of any other; there is a place for all in the body and none can take another's place.

Paul goes on to say as much in the latter half of 1 Corinthians 12. There are two attitudes, he says, which are completely eliminated by the fact of spiritual gifts. One is self-depreciation.

If the foot should say, "Because I am not a hand, I do not belong to the body," that would not make it any less a part of the body. And if the ear should say, "Because I am not an eye, I do not belong to the body," that would not make it any less a part of the body (vv. 15,16).

This completely destroys the argument of the Christian who says, "There's nothing I can do; others have gifts and abilities but since I can't do what they do I must not be of much use in the church." Paul's conclusion to this line of argument is: *But as it is, God arranged the organs in the body, each one of them, as he chose* (v. 18).

On the other hand, there is no room for self-sufficiency:

The eye cannot say to the hand, "I have no need of you." Nor again the head to the feet, "I have no need of you." On the contrary, the parts of the body which seem to be weaker are indispensable, and those parts of the body which we think less honorable we invest with the greater honor, and our unpresentable parts are treated with greater modesty, which our more presentable parts do not require (vv. 21-24).

No member of the body has the right to look down on or despise the ministry of another. We need each other and that desperately. No Christian, or group of Christians, can do the task alone. No denomination constitutes the whole body, and no Christian organization possesses all the gifts in the variety of combinations necessary to do the work God wants done today. We are members one of another and it is time we took these words seriously and began to act like one harmonious body again.

The gifts of the Spirit are not only for use within the church. They are for the world as well. Some who have the gift of teaching ought to be exercising it in their homes. Some who have the gift of helping ought to be using it in the office, the shop, or wherever they are. Some who have the gift of wisdom should be putting it to work wherever they touch people. These gifts are intended for all of life. Remember that the ministry of the body is the ministry of Jesus Christ, at work in human society. Christ loves this world and the men and women in it. He loves the homeless, pathetic derelicts who drift up and down the streets of our big cities in increasing numbers. He loves the narcotics victims, the alcoholics, the devotees of sex perversions, the acid heads and prostitutes. He loves the hard-driving, hardheaded business men who have made a god of success and have fallen for the illusion that wealth means happiness. He loves them all and wants to reach them—through his body. That's why he has equipped it with gifts, and filled it with his life.

CHAPTER SIX

According to the Power

In this chapter we face a most important question. How is the church expected to accomplish its task of influencing society? By what power is it to operate? Upon what resource does it rely? Is it to be by some wonder-working, dramatic display of miracles? Is it to be by the power of numbers—getting so many people together to vote the same way and thus exert pressure upon legislatures to change society by new and more just laws? Is this the real power of the church? Or is it by agitating for change by joining picket lines, sit-ins, walkouts or rise-ups? Does the power of the church perhaps come from the holding of conventions devoted to discussions of various issues and issuing pronouncements and resolutions?

61

You will note that in writing to the Ephesians the apostle Paul does not suggest any of these activities. Rather the apostle reminds us that the fundamental secret of the operation of the church is that each true Christian has a gift and is expected to operate that gift or cluster of gifts in the power provided by Jesus Christ. This is the way he puts it:

> But grace was given to each of us according to the measure of Christ's gift. Therefore it is said, "When he ascended on high he led a host of captives, and he gave gifts to men." (In saying, "He ascended," what does it mean but that he had also descended into the lower parts of the earth? He who descended is he who also ascended far above all the heavens, that he might fill all things) (Eph. 4:7-10).

We need to note immediately that there are two kinds of gifts mentioned in verse 7. One, Paul calls the measure of the other. *But grace (that is the first gift) was given to each of us, according to the measure of Christ's gift* (or more literally, the gift of Christ—the second gift). This "gift of Christ" is the more basic gift of the two and refers to Christ himself. That is, Paul is not here talking about something which Christ gives to us, but something God has given us, which is Christ. The gift is Christ himself. As Paul says in 2 Corinthians 9:15, *Thanks be to God for his inexpressible gift!* Because Christ is made known to us by the presence of the Holy Spirit in our lives it is equally proper to call this the gift of the Holy Spirit, as the apostle Peter does in Acts 2:38:

> And Peter said to them, "Repent, and be baptized every one of you in the name of Jesus Christ for the forgiveness of your sins; and you shall receive the gift of the Holy Spirit."

Thus the basic gift is the indwelling of the Spirit of Christ within each believer. That is what makes anyone a Christian. Paul says to the Romans, *Any one who does not have the Spirit of Christ does not belong to him* (Rom. 8:9). He may be religious and a member of a church, faithfully attending all meetings and fulfilling all obligations, but if he does not have the Spirit living within he is not one of Christ's. That is the essential.

There is also the special "grace" mentioned here which is the gift of the Spirit to each Christian as a special ability or capacity for service. We have examined these in detail. It is this gift (or cluster of gifts) which must be exercised *according to the measure of Christ's gift*.

Christ's Triumphal March

At this point (Eph. 4:7,8) we must ask: Why does the apostle tie this immediately to Christ's ascension and his previous descent to earth? Why does he here quote from Psalm 68, verse 18, the words: *When he ascended on high he led a host of captives, and he gave gifts to men*? He seems to put great emphasis on Christ's triumphal march, leading a host of captives in his train. What is the reason for it?

It is obvious that these verses from the Psalm are intended to amplify and explain the phrase, *according to the measure of the gift of Christ*. A gift is one thing, the power to use it is quite another. Now Paul is bringing these two together. Graces, he says, are given to us to use according to the measure of power available to us. And that power is the life of a risen and enthroned Lord, living within us by means of his Spirit.

It is helpful to ask, what kind of power is needed to operate the gift which God has given you? Do you need the power of a strong personality? There are evidently many who think so. Many Christians are not using the gift God has given them because they think it requires a strong personality to do so. If they have an outgoing, extroverted personality they can expect to be used of God, but not otherwise. If that, then, is the power that is required, it is obvious that there are many who never stand a chance since they simply are not extroverts. And even those who are often find occasions when they do not feel particularly outgoing.

Well then, is it the power of positive thinking that is required? We read much about this today. Do we need to read certain books and develop our inner attitudes in such a way that we are always thinking positively and never negatively, and thus we can become useful to Jesus Christ? If that is the kind of power that is needed, it is obvious that it is never available if we happen to be in a depressed or negative mood. Positive thinking is nothing more than wishful thinking if the facts of a situation are contrary to what we desire. While, in general, it is good to be optimistic, that optimism must have some basis in fact to be of any help at all.

Then is it the power of a keen intellect that is needed? Must we all seek to have a well-trained, educated mind, sharpened and honed to the highest degree by the resources of modern knowledge? But some are born with a low IQ and no amount of knowledge will increase it. Others do not have, and never will have, the advantage of training and education. Are they shut away from being of use to the Spirit of God by these disadvantages? It is evident that we need a power that is different from any of the ones mentioned and is superior to all circumstances. We need power that is not affected by education, either the presence of it or the lack of it. We need power that is independent of moods or feelings.

That is precisely the kind of power which the apostle is referring to when he speaks of the ascension and triumphal appearance of Christ before the throne of God that he might give gifts to men. It is the power of a risen Lord, the power of resurrection! Paul coveted this highly for himself, for he cries out in his Philippian letter, *that I may know him and the power of his resurrection* (Phil. 3:10). Because of the descent of Christ to earth (his incarnation), and his ascent again to the throne of power after his resurrection, that remarkable power is now available to Christians.

It took his descent from glory down to this earth, all the pain, anguish, heartache and sorrow of the cross, and finally a resurrection from the dead and an ascension in triumph into the heavens to receive gifts from the Father before it was possible for him to give those gifts to you. A spiritual gift is no common thing. As we have seen, it is not merely a natural talent. It is a divinely given ability requiring resurrection power to exercise it. The gifts, therefore, which Christ has given you are the most precious you could ever have.

Cord and Plug

These spiritual gifts are like so many electrical appliances. What a variety of appliances are available today. There are electric toasters, toothbrushes, mixers, irons, razors, dishwashers, and a host of others. I even saw an advertisement one day for an electric shoestring tier! I may be ready for that myself in a few more years! But if you look carefully at these electrical appliances you will see that though they are vastly different in their function there is one thing they all have in common: they all have a cord with a plug at the end. They are all designed to utilize the same power! No matter how different the appliance may be, the power required is the same for all.

But it is not utilized to the same extent. Each appliance uses its own specific amount of power. Some are marked for 50 watts, some use 100 watts, some only 20 or less, while others may require 1500 or more. The degree of power that is required to operate the appliance is usually stamped on each. At wedding showers young couples are often given many different electrical appliances. As they go through their gifts, noting the many varieties, they might well say, "Appliances were given to us to use according to the measure of the power available."

The early Christians knew the secret of living by resurrection power and nothing else will account for the amazing effect they had upon the world of their day. They did not try to borrow power from the world, for they found they had all they could possibly need, available continuously from a risen, triumphant Lord. Thus Paul writes in Ephesians 3:20,21: *Now to him who by the power at work within us is able to do far more abundantly than all that we ask or think . . . be glory in the church.*

Paul claims this for himself as well: *Of this gospel I was made a minister according to the gift of God's grace [the grace, or spiritual gift given to him] which was given me by the working of his power* (Eph. 3:7). The only limit the apostle ever found to this resurrection power was the limit of his faith to receive it. As faith grew his effectiveness grew. He did not always see the results himself but he knew they were always there, for resurrection power can never fail.

Like No Other

We must understand that resurrection power is like no other power on earth. It is unique, and has no possible rival. For one thing, it is the kind of power that operates in the midst of death. It works when everything around it is dull, dead and barren. It works best in the midst of a cemetery, for that is where it was first demonstrated. When Jesus Christ was resurrected he came out from among the dead. Therefore, if you learn

66

to live by resurrection power you can be alive and vital when everything and everyone around you is dead and lifeless.

Furthermore, resurrection power makes no noise. Other kinds of power that we know usually make some kind of sound: they pound, pulsate, throb, hum, buzz, explode, or roar. But resurrection power is quite silent. Without any display or ostentation it quietly accomplishes its purpose though there is nothing audible or visible to mark it. When a Christian is living by resurrection power he does not advertise it or seek to dazzle others by its display. His effect upon others is quiet and unobserved at first, but soon there are evident changes that mark the inevitable effect of resurrection power at work: the return of life, vitality, excitement and joy to an individual or situation. In that marvelous way God has of illustrating spiritual truth in nature, there is a picture of this kind of power at work in every returning springtime. Out of the cold, barren, death of winter, God brings new life, color, warmth, and glory by means of a quiet, invisible force which gradually transforms the whole landscape into a fairyland of beauty.

Resurrection power is also irresistible. It cannot be thwarted or turned aside. It takes absolutely no account of any obstacles thrown into its path, except to use them for further opportunities to advance its cause. When Jesus came bursting from the grave he paid not the slightest attention to the obstacles man had placed in his way. There was a large stone in front of his tomb; he passed through it. He himself was wrapped in yard after yard of linen cloth; he left the graveclothes undisturbed behind him. There were Roman guards in front of his tomb; he ignored them. He took not the slightest notice of the decrees of Caesar or the orders of Pilate or the fulminations of the Jewish priests.

When Paul wrote to the Philippians from his imprisonment in Rome he said:

I want you to know, brethren, that what has happened to me has really served to advance the gospel, so that it has become known throughout the whole praetorian guard and to all the rest that my imprisonment is for Christ (Phil. 1:12,13). Every effort being made to stop the gospel was really advancing it. Because Paul had learned to depend on the power of Christ's resurrection he was not in the least disturbed by apparent setbacks. He did not rely upon his own cleverness or upon the influence and intervention of others, but solely upon the ability of a risen Lord to bring about his will in spite of man's deliberate attempts to forestall it.

Resurrection power needs no props or support. It does not borrow from any other source, though it uses other forms of power as its instrument. It does not even require a cup of coffee to get started in the morning! There is absolutely nothing else like it anywhere in the universe.

Available by Faith

It is available to every true Christian by faith. Faith is a human response to a divine promise. Faith is a sense of expectation, a quiet trust that another will do exactly as he said he would do. Abraham *grew strong in his faith as he gave glory to God, fully convinced that God was able to do what he had promised* (Rom. 4:20,21). Faith has nothing to do with feelings, takes no account of moods or physical conditions, because it does not look to any human for help but to God alone.

Therefore, the Christian, who believes that a risen Jesus Christ now lives in him, confidently expects Christ to be at work in whatever he does to add the divine "plus" that marks the presence of resurrection power. Christ will not necessarily be felt, but he will be present. He will make ordinary words produce extraordinary results: He will take common relationships and transform them into uncommon accomplishments. He will do exactly as he promised: *exceeding abundantly above all that is asked or thought* not according to man's time schedule but according to God's.

Surely this is the missing note in today's church activity. The church is still the church, still the body of Christ, but it has been brainwashed by the world to the point that it has forgotten the divine provision for reaching the world. It will never again affect the world as it did in the first century until individual Christians begin to utilize the gifts God has given them in the power of a resurrected Lord. This should be the most important thing in the world to each Christian—more important than his standard of living, his success in business, his desire to travel or find romance, or whatever.

Paul puts the case clearly in Romans 13:

The night is far gone, the day is at hand. Let us then cast off the works of darkness and put on the armor of light; let us conduct ourselves becomingly as in the day, not in reveling and drunkenness, not in debauchery and licentiousness, not in quarreling and jealousy. But put on the Lord Jesus Christ, and make no provision for the flesh, to gratify its desires (Rom. 13:12-14).

In the next chapter we shall learn just how pastors and other church leaders fit into this divine provision for the operation of Christ's body, the church. Be prepared for some surprises.

CHAPTER SEVEN

How the Body Works

In his letter to the Ephesian Christians the apostle Paul uses two great figures for the church. As we have seen, he likens it to a human body of flesh and bones, made up of many members articulated and coordinated together. He also likens it to a building which he describes as growing through the centuries to be a habitation for God through the Spirit. Here he seems to mix his metaphors for he speaks of a building growing. Now buildings don't grow, though bodies do, but the apostle perhaps deliberately puts it this way in order that we might capture the thought of the church as something living. Sometimes we unconsciously mix metaphors in the same way, like, "You buttered your bread, now lie in it!"

When Paul speaks of the church as a body he makes

clear that no one joins that body except by a new birth, through faith in Jesus Christ. There is no other way into this body. Once he has become a part of that body, every member has a contribution to make. As each member works at what God has given him to do, the whole body functions as intended. When Paul describes the church as a building he makes clear that it is a living, growing building. Every Christian is a stone added to that building, a "living stone" as Peter calls him in his first letter. Each is a vital part of the great temple which the Holy Spirit is building as a habitation for God. We can never understand the church till we accept that picture. Many people, seeking to discover God today, say that he is dead. The trouble is, they do not know his present address. They don't know where he lives. But he is very much at home in his body, the building made for him by the Holy Spirit.

If we think of the church as a body, then in Ephesians 4 we are viewing the physiology of that body—how the organs operate, how the various members are coordinated to do one thing. If we think of the church as a building, then we are considering the blueprints, the architecture, of the building. But whether the church is regarded as a body or a building, there are four ministries, or functions, within it which are so universally needed and so mutually shared that we must consider them independently from the other gifts which Christ gives to his church. These four are now brought before us by the apostle in verses 11 and 12:

His gifts were that some should be apostles, some prophets, some evangelists, some pastors and teachers, for the equipment of the saints, for the work of ministry, for building up of the body of Christ.

These four—apostles, prophets, evangelists, and pastor-teachers—are the gifts we reserved for later discussion (chapter 4) and are part of the gifts which a risen

71

Lord imparted to men. They constitute what we shall call "support gifts" as contrasted with the "service" and "sign" gifts previously considered from 1 Corinthians 12 and Romans 12. These four relate to the whole body of Christ very much as the major systems relate to the physical body. There are, within the human body, four major systems upon which the entire body is dependent for proper functioning: the skeletal and muscular framework, the nervous, the digestive and the circulatory systems. There are other systems in the body which are not essential for life itself (such as the reproductive system) but these four are. In a most remarkable way they correspond to the four support ministries within the body of Christ.

Bones and Muscles

First, there is the basic structural system of bones and muscles. This gives the body its fundamental support and makes possible mobility and activity. We would all be nothing but rolling masses of gelatine if it were not for the bones and muscles. This clearly corresponds to the apostles and their function in the body of Christ. Their work was foundational, skeletal. They formed the basic structure which made the body of Christ assume the particular form it has.

To revert for a moment to the figure of the church as a building there is a clear word from the apostle concerning the function of the apostles and prophets. In Ephesians 2:10,20 he says,

So then you are no longer strangers and sojourners, but you are fellow citizens with the saints and members of the household of God, built upon the foundation of the apostles and prophets, Christ Jesus himself being the cornerstone.

The foundation of the church is Jesus Christ, as Paul declared to the Corinthians, *For no other foundation can any one lay than that which is laid, which is Jesus Christ* (1 Cor. 3:11), and the primary work of an apostle was to declare the whole body of truth concerning Jesus Christ. That is the foundation. What the apostles say about Jesus Christ is the foundation of the church, and what they said about Jesus Christ is recorded for us in the New Testament. That book is written by the apostles and prophets, and the church rests squarely upon that foundation.

How does one get into the church? By believing the truth about Jesus Christ (and believing means more than intellectual assent; it is a commitment of the will as well). It is only as the church rests upon this foundation of the faith, as taught by the apostles, that there is any certainty or strength. Today many are straying from the foundation and as a result they have lost any note of authority or assurance. Merely human viewpoints or opinions do not change the foundation. Modern knowledge, or the discoveries of science, will not alter it. Our ultimate concern is what the apostles taught. That is the greatest revelation of reality which we possess, *the truth [as it] is in Jesus* (Eph. 4:21).

Men who are in the construction business know that a foundation is of the utmost importance. You do not take risks with a foundation. You lay it squarely, securely, and strongly, for the whole building is going to rest on that foundation and will derive its strength from the character of the foundation. The same thing is true of the church. The Lord Jesus made very clear that if a man builds on the wrong foundation he is in trouble. One man may build his house on the sand and the house may look very beautiful, very impressive, but when the storms come, it falls. Another man may build on the rock and his house will stand in the storm. It is the foundation which makes all the difference.

Jesus himself is the one who named the apostles. We

have the record in the Gospels of the Lord calling twelve men to be "with him." That was their primary characteristic as apostles, men who had been with Jesus. He sent them out in a specialized ministry. (The word "apostle" means one sent out or one sent forth.) The Twelve had a special commission and a special authority. As you follow their ministry you recognize that they possessed an authoritative word. Wherever they went they spoke with authority. They were impressed with this themselves. They came back to Jesus and told him how they rejoiced to discover that the demons were subject to them. When they spoke the word they had authority and that word of authority is the special mark of an apostle.

Paul, of course, was a special apostle, chosen by Jesus after his resurrection. He did not obtain his ministry from the Twelve but directly from the Lord himself, though what he taught and preached was in no sense different from what the Twelve proclaimed.

The apostolic gift is still being given today, though in a secondary sense. There is no new truth to be added to the Scriptures, but the body of truth which we have is to be taken by those who have an apostolic gift and imparted to new churches wherever they may begin. It is part of the apostolic gift to start new churches. We call those who do this "pioneer missionaries" today. Through the course of church history there have been many such secondary apostles, as Adoniram Judson in Burma, William Carey in India, Hudson Taylor in China, etc. These were men who had the apostolic gift and were made responsible for imparting the whole faith to new churches.

To return to the figure of the body, this apostolic system of truth is the bones and muscles of the church. There is no other line of truth about Jesus Christ. There is no other information which can come to us

74

about Jesus than what the apostles have given. There is nothing else. If there seems to be, then, as Paul says to the Galatians, "it is another gospel." It is something different (see Acts 4:12; Gal. 1:7). Here is the skeleton of the body, and upon this the church is built and from this comes its strength.

Galvanized into Action

Linked with the skeletal system in the human body is the nervous system. It is the means by which the bones and muscles are stimulated to activity, galvanized into action. The nervous system is the directive system. It is linked directly to the head, and from there it conveys messages to every part of the body. This system corresponds to the work of prophets in the body of Christ.

A prophet is essentially a man who speaks for God, who unfolds the mind of God. In the early church, before the New Testament was written down, prophets spoke directly by the inspiration of the Holy Spirit, uttering the truths that are now recorded in the New Testament. They unfolded what God taught, and thus the body was motivated, galvanized into activity. Men such as Mark, Luke, James, and Jude were not themselves apostles but they were associated with the apostles in the writing of the New Testament.

The gift of a prophet differs from that of an apostle: The apostle gives an authoritative declaration of the whole body of truth concerning Jesus Christ; but the prophet interprets that authoritative word and explains the truth so that it becomes very clear, vital, and compelling. The very word "prophet" suggests this. It derives from a Greek root which means "to cause to shine," and is linked with the prefix "pro" which means "before." Thus a prophet is one who stands before and causes the word of the apostle to shine. That is beauti-

75

fully reflected in Peter's second letter when he says, *We have the prophetic word made more sure. You will do well to pay attention to this as to a lamp shining in a dark place* (2 Pet. 1:19). Paul also says in 1 Corinthians 14, *He who prophesies speaks to men for their upbuilding and encouragement and consolation* (v. 3).

The church owes much to the ministry of prophets. Not only were parts of the Scriptures given to us by prophets but the great theologians and preachers of the church have been men with prophetic gifts. Men such as Martin Luther, John Calvin, John Wesley, and the founders of other denominations have been prophets, and many pastors and Bible teachers today have prophetic gifts. Usually men who speak at conferences are speaking as prophets, making the truth clear, shining, and gripping. They differ from teachers in that the prophet tends more to deal with the great sweeping principles of Scripture and reality, leaving the development of more specific areas to the teacher.

From Food to Flesh

The third support ministry within the body of Christ is the evangelist. He is linked with the work of the pastor-teacher. Evangelists and teaching pastors work together just as the apostles and prophets work together. Evangelists are men and women with a special gift of communicating the gospel in relevant terms to those who are not yet Christians. Since the evangelist is primarily responsible for the numerical growth of the body of Christ his ministry corresponds to the digestive system within the human body which takes food which is quite unlike flesh and transforms it into flesh and bones, making it a living part of the body.

All Christians are expected to evangelize, but not all have the gift of an evangelist. Christians are to evangelize as witnesses, but a witness is different than an

76

evangelist. Any individual Christian should be able to relate what happened to him in becoming a Christian; to give a simple testimonial of what Jesus Christ has done for him. This is as easy as talking about any other meaningful experience. If you can talk about how wonderful your husband is, or your wife, or your children or grandchildren, you can also witness for Christ. To talk about your Christian experience simply and naturally is Christian witnessing. But an evangelist goes further. He knows how to explain the why and how of the great redeeming story of Jesus Christ. He is able to proclaim the truth which results in new birth. He is forever dealing with the truth that God has not left man in a hopeless condition but has made a way, at great and incredible cost, by which men and women involved in an endless battle against the deteriorating forces of life, can be freed, given a new start and a new basis for the battle. That is the work of an evangelist.

The evangelist's task is not to go about denouncing sin. He may call people's attention to that which is creating so much misery and heartache in their lives, but his work is not to denounce them in their sin. He is not to thunder away at people, telling them what miserable creatures they are and how God is waiting to strike them with thunderbolts of judgment. He is not to expose the horrors of hellfire and hang sinners over it until they writhe and tremble. That is not the calling of the evangelist. If it needs to be done at all, that is the work of the prophet. The evangelist's task is to tell of the overwhelming grace of God and the overpowering love of a heavenly Father who is calling men and women back to himself and offering to set their twisted lives straight through the redeeming work of Jesus Christ.

Many Christians today possess the gift of an evangelist, both men and women. Evangelism can be done

77

anywhere. It is not restricted to mass meetings, such as in the great Billy Graham crusades, though Graham's ministry is also true evangelism. The gift of an evangelist can be exercised toward a single individual, as is clear in the book of Acts when Philip the evangelist spoke to the Ethiopian eunuch as he was riding along in a chariot and told him of the saving grace of Jesus Christ.

Feeding and Cleansing

The fourth great system within the physical body upon which the body is totally dependent for life is the circulatory system with its veins and arteries linked to the heart and lungs to distribute food and oxygen to every part of the body, and take away the accumulated wastes. Obviously this corresponds to the work of teaching pastors within the body of Christ who are there to maintain the life of the body by feeding and cleansing it and preserving its life in vigor and vitality.

The word "pastor" means a shepherd. The pastor is also called in the Scriptures an elder, as well as overseer or bishop. These last two are the same Greek word, translated in two different ways. "Bishop" is the English translation of *episcopus*, which literally means an overseer. Elders or bishops were always limited to one locality, one church, in New Testament days. A man who was an elder or pastor in one church was not also an elder in another place.

Nor were these men who always devoted their full time to ministry. Certain of the elders were called ruling elders and they were often supported by the church to devote full time to their work, though this was not always the case. There were also others who were elders but were not called ruling elders. These included anyone who did shepherding work within the church. Today these would be involved as Sunday

78

School teachers, home Bible class leaders, and young people's leaders. Many Christians have the gift of pastor-teacher whether they are working at it full time or not.

The ruling elders correspond most closely to the present concept of a pastor, but in the early church there was never a single pastor or elder but always several. They were to be teachers and administrators, but not, as Peter says, *as domineering over those in your charge*. (1 Pet. 5:3). In other words, they are not to be church bosses. They are not to act as the final authority within the church so that whatever they say goes. Jesus himself taught this. Mark records that Jesus called the disciples to him and said, *You know that those who are supposed to rule over the Gentiles lord it over them, and their great men exercise authority over them. But it shall not be so among you* (Mark 10:42, 43).

The pastors of the churches therefore are not to exercise their authority as bosses but as examples. When they themselves obey the word others will be motivated to follow, but if the teaching pastors do not practice what they preach they have no other authority. Their authority derives from their spirituality and if they lose their spirituality they also lose their authority. It is not the office that gives a pastor the right to rule—it is the man and his gift before God. This question of a pastor's authority is so important and so misunderstood among the churches that I want to take the time here to comment further on how the Scriptures view the matter.

No Command Structure

Authority among Christians is not derived from the same source as worldly authority, nor is it to be exercised in the same manner. The world's view of authority places men *over* one another, as in a military command structure, a business executive hierarchy or a governmental system. This is as it should be. Urged by the competitiveness created by the Fall, and faced with the rebelliousness and ruthlessness of sinful human nature, the world could not function without the use of command structures and executive decision.

But as Jesus carefully stated, *it shall not be so among you*. Disciples are always in a different relationship to one another than worldlings are. Christians are brothers and sisters, children of one Father and members one of another. Jesus put it clearly in Matthew 23:8, *You have one teacher, and you are all brethren*.

Throughout twenty centuries the church has virtually ignored these words. Probably with the best of intentions, it has repeatedly borrowed the authority structures of the world, changed the names of executives from kings, generals, captains, presidents, governors, secretaries, heads and chiefs to popes, patriarchs, bishops, stewards, deacons, pastors and elders, and gone merrily on its way, lording it *over* the brethren and thus destroying the model of servanthood which our Lord intended.

In most churches today an unthinking acceptance has been given to the idea that the pastor is the final voice of authority in both doctrine and practice, and that he is the executive officer of the church with respect to administration. But surely, if a pope over the whole church is bad, a pope in every church is no better!

But if the church is not to imitate the world in this matter, what is it to do? Leadership must certainly be exercised within the church and there must be some form of authority. The question is answered in Jesus' words, *You have one teacher*. All too long churches have behaved as if Jesus were far away in heaven and he has left it up to church leaders to make their own decisions and run their own affairs. But Jesus himself had assured them in giving the Great Commission, *Lo, I am with you always, to the close of the age.* And in Matthew 18:20 he reiterated, *Where two or three are gathered in my name, there am I in the midst of them.* Clearly this indicates that he is present not only in the church as a whole but in every local church as well. It is Jesus himself, therefore, who is the ultimate authority within every body of Christians and he is quite prepared to exercise his authority through the instrument he himself has ordained—the eldership.

The task of the elders is not to run the church themselves but to determine how the Lord in their midst wishes to run his church. Much of this he has already made known through the Scriptures which describe the impartation and exercise of spiritual gifts, the availability of resurrection power and the responsibility of believers to bear one another's burdens, confess sins to one another, teach, admonish and reprove one another, and witness to and serve the needs of a hurting world.

The Mind of the Spirit

In the day-to-day decisions which every church faces, elders are to seek and find the mind of the Lord through an uncoerced unanimity, reached after thorough and biblically-related discussion. Thus, ultimate authority, even in practical matters, is vested in the Lord and in no one else. This is what the book of Acts reveals in its description of the initiative actions of the Holy Spirit who obviously planned and ordered the evangelizing strategy of the early church (Acts 8; 13; etc.). The elders sought the mind of the Spirit and, when it was made clear to them, they acted with unity of thought and purpose. (*For it has seemed good to the Holy Spirit and to us to lay upon you no greater burden,* Acts 15:28.) The authority, therefore, was not the authority of men but of God and it was expressed not through men, acting as individuals, but through the collective, united agreement of men whom the Spirit had led to eldership (see Acts 20:28).

The point is: No one man is the sole expression of the mind of the Spirit; no individual has authority from God to direct the affairs of the church. A plurality of elders is necessary as a safeguard to the all-too-human tendency to play God over other people. Even then, the authority exercised is not one of domination and arbitrary decree over anyone. The ability of a servant to influence anyone else does not lie in ordering someone around but in obtaining their voluntary consent. This is the nature of all authority among Christians, even that of the Lord himself! He does not force our obedience, but obtains it by love, expressed either in circumstantial discipline or by awakening gratitude through the meeting of our desperate needs.

The true authority of elders and other leaders in the church is that of respect, aroused by their own loving and godly example. This is the force of two verses which are often cited by those who claim a unique authority of pastors over church members. The first is found in 1 Thessalonians 5:12,13, *But we beseech you, brethren, to respect those who labor among you, and are over you in the Lord and admonish you, and to esteem them very highly in love because of their work.* The key phrase is *and are over you in the Lord;* the Greek word in question is *prohistamenous.* Though this is translated "over you" in both the *Revised Standard Version* and *King James Version*, the word itself contains no implication of being over another. The *New English Bible* more properly renders it, *and in the Lord's fellowship are your leaders and counsellors.* The thought in the word is that of "standing before" others, not of "ruling over" them. It is the common word for leadership. Leaders can lead only if they are able to persuade some to follow.

Another verse used to support command authority is Hebrews 13:17, which the *Revised Standard Version* renders, *Obey your leaders and submit to them; for they are keeping watch over your souls, as men who will have to give account.* The imperative translated "obey" is from the word *peitho*, to persuade. In the middle voice, used here, Thayer's lexicon gives its meaning as "to suffer one's self to be persuaded." Again there is no thought of a right to command someone against his will. But the clear thrust is that leaders are persuaders whose ability to persuade arises not from a smooth tongue or a dominant personality but from a personal walk which evokes respect.

Why Change Now?

At this point many may be tempted to say, "What difference does it make? After all, the pattern of command authority is too widely established to alter now, and besides, many churches seem to be doing all right as it is; why try to change now?"

In response, consider the following:

1. The Bible indicates that any deviation from the divine plan inevitably produces weakness, division, strife, increasing fruitlessness and, ultimately, death. The present low state of many churches is testimony to the effects of ignoring, over a long period of time, God's way of working.

2. A command structure of authority in the church deprives the world of any model or demonstration of a different way of life than the one it already lives by. Worldlings see no difference in the church and can see no reason why they should change and believe.

3. A command authority inevitably produces resentment, repression, exploitation and, finally, rebellion.

It is law, which Scripture assures us can never redeem or restore us, but which must, by its very nature, condemn and repress.

4. The desire of the Lord Jesus to show to the world a wholly new form of authority which is consistent with grace, not law, is nullified by a command structure among Christians, and the gospel of dying-to-live is denied before it is proclaimed. This means that God is robbed of his glory and distorted before the watching world. Nothing could be more serious than this!

Note that each of the four support ministries described earlier has to do with the word of God. The first two—apostles and prophets—are concerned with originating and expounding the word, while the last two—evangelists and pastor-teachers—are concerned with applying the word to individual lives. The evangelist deals with the beginning of Christian life while the teaching pastor is involved with the development and growth of that life. Evangelists are basically obstetricians, having to do with birth, while teaching pastors are pediatricians, having to do with diet and diseases and the need for fresh air and exercise.

To return to the figure of a building, the evangelist is the quarryman who digs out the rock, cuts it loose from its basic structure, and hews it to a rough approximation of its ultimate size. The pastor-teacher then is the stone mason who shapes the rock, fitting it into the building in its proper place according to the blueprint of the great architect.

When we compare the present-day churches to the original blueprint it is strikingly apparent that many deviations have been permitted which have been detrimental to the life of the church. Through the centuries the church gradually turned away from the simple provisions which made it such a powerful and compelling force in its early years, and there came in terrible distortions from which we are suffering greatly today. The popular thinking fastened upon the building as the identifying symbol of the church and emphasis was put upon great imposing structures and massive cathedrals. In the beginning, "working in the church" meant to exercise a gift or perform a ministry among Christian people wherever they were, but gradually it came to mean doing some religious act within a building.

Along with this there came a gradual transfer of responsibility from the people to what was termed "the clergy," which is a term derived from the Latin *clericus* meaning a priest. The scriptural concept that every believer is a priest before God was gradually lost and a special body of super-Christians emerged who were looked to for practically everything and so came to be termed "the ministry." Now it is most apparent from Ephesians 4 that all Christians are "in the ministry." The proper task of the four support ministries we have been examining is to train, motivate, and undergird the people to do the work of the ministry.

When the ministry was thus left to the professionals there was nothing left for the people to do other than come to church and listen. They were told that it was their responsibility to bring the world into the church building to hear the pastor preach the gospel. Soon Christianity became nothing but a spectator sport, very much akin to the definition of football—twenty-two men down on the field, desperately in need of rest, and twenty thousand in the grandstands, desperately in need of exercise!

This unbiblical distortion has placed pastors under an unbearable burden. They have proved completely unequal to the task of evangelizing the world, counseling the distressed and brokenhearted, ministering to the poor and needy, relieving the oppressed and afflicted, expounding the Scriptures, and challenging the entrenched forces of evil in an increasingly darkened world. They were never meant to do it. To even attempt it is to end up frustrated, exhausted, and emotionally drained.

Further, this distortion has resulted in a sadly impoverished church which has made little impact on the world and increasingly withdraws into impotent isolation. Nothing is more desperately needed than to return to the dynamic of the early church. We can no longer defend our ivy-clad traditions which leave no room for this New Testament pattern. Pastors, particularly, must restore to the people the ministry which was taken from them with the best of intentions.

Again it is the entire body of believers who must attempt the work of the ministry, equipped and guided by gifted men who are able to expound and apply the Scriptures with such wisdom that even the least believer discovers and begins to exercise the gift or gifts the Holy Spirit has given him. The whole body then stirs with resurrection power. Boldness and power again become the trademarks of the church of Jesus Christ.

CHAPTER EIGHT

Shaping Up the Saints

Throughout the Christian centuries no principle of church life has proved more revolutionary (and therefore, more bitterly fought) than the declaration of Ephesians 4 that the ultimate work of the church in the world is to be done by the saints—plain, ordinary, Christians—and not by a professional clergy or a few select laymen. We must never lose the impact of the apostle Paul's statement that apostles, prophets, evangelists, and pastor-teachers exist *for the equipment of the saints, for the work of ministry, for building up of the body of Christ* (Eph. 4:12).

Perhaps this can be made clearer if we diagram verses 11 and 12 in the following manner:

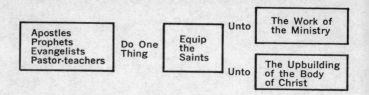

Note that neither the apostles and prophets nor the evangelists and pastor-teachers are expected to do the work of the ministry, or even to build up the body of Christ. Those tasks are to be done only by the people, the ordinary, plain vanilla Christians we mentioned above. The four offices of apostle, prophet, evangelist, and pastor-teacher exist for but one function: that of equipping the common Christians to do the tasks which are assigned to them.

So let's take a closer look at the word "equipping." What does this mean and how is it done? In the original Greek the word is *katartismon*, from which we get our English word, "artisan"—an artist or craftsman, someone who works with his hands to make or build things. It is a special point of interest that this word first appears in the New Testament in connection with the calling of the disciples. As Jesus walked along the Sea of Galilee, he saw two pairs of brothers, Peter and Andrew and James and John, sitting in a boat busily engaged in doing something. What were they doing? They were mending their nets. The word "mending" is the word translated in Ephesians 4 as "equipping." They were equipping their nets by mending them. They were getting them ready for action, fixing them up, preparing them.

Mending the Saints

This suggests, therefore, that the role of the four support gifts within the church is essentially that of

88

mending the saints, getting them ready for action. The word is also translated as "fitting them out" or "preparing." The Greek authority, J. H. Thayer, says it means "to make one what he ought to be." Perhaps the nearest modern equivalent is "to shape up." The ultimate aim of apostles, prophets, evangelists, and pastor-teachers is the shaping up of the saints to do the work of the ministry.

A moment's thought will make clear that the instrument to be used by the four support gifts in equipping the saints is the word of God. Obviously, all four support ministries relate somehow to that word. The apostles and prophets originated and expounded it. As we have noted, they laid the foundations upon which the whole church must rest. The ministry of the apostles is still available to us through the written New Testament, and prophets are still given by the Holy Spirit to the churches to unfold the word of the apostles and make it clear and powerful.

Evangelists and pastor-teachers are to proclaim and apply the word. Evangelists move about, some more widely than others, telling the great historic facts of what God has done for man in Jesus Christ, and describing what will result in the life of anyone who believes these facts. They also have a responsibility to take with them younger Christians who share the gift of an evangelist and to train them in how to proclaim the good news effectively in the power of a risen Lord.

The task of the pastor-teacher is to use the word of God to cleanse and feed the flock. The early church clearly understood that the word of God was the instrument of growth in the lives of Christians. Paul once spoke to the very elders to whom this Ephesian letter is addressed and said to them:

And now I commend you to God and to the word of his grace, which is able to build you up and to give

you the inheritance among all those who are sanctified
(Acts 20:32). And again, at the close of his career, he
wrote to his son in the faith, young Timothy, and
urged him to teach the inspired Scriptures which were
given, *that the man of God may be complete, equipped
for every good work.* If pastors and teachers deliberately
ignore this divinely-provided instrument, it is no wonder
that the saints remain unequipped for their tasks and
various substitute activities must be found to keep them
occupied.

The Whole Truth

This teaching of the truth of the word of God is
what Peter calls, *feeding the flock of God which is
among you* (1 Pet. 5:2). The word can both feed (Heb.
5:12,13, 1 Pet. 2:2), and cleanse (John 15:3; Eph.
5:26), and the true pastor will constantly be using it to
do both. He will seek to teach the whole truth of God.
There is no better means to do this than the expository
preaching of the whole Bible. The expository method
of teaching or preaching is to go through a book, or a
section of a book of the Bible, leaving out nothing,
commenting on everything, touching it all. That will
keep truth in balance.

The prophet Isaiah says that this was the way Scripture was originally given. *Precept upon precept, precept upon precept, line upon line, line upon line, here
a little, there a little.* (Isa. 28:13). You won't find in
the Bible a chapter on evil and another on morals and
another on baptism, etc. These subjects are all woven
together in a delightful sanity of balance. One can
never take a sizable section of the word of God and
comment on it without presenting truth in balance. It
is truth in balance which does the trick of equipping
the saints.

The business of preaching is, as someone has well

90

put it, "to comfort the disturbed and disturb the comfortable." The truth is very comforting and enlightening, but it also ought to get under our collars, and into our hearts, and disturb us greatly at times. Only the word of God can do this. It is the pounding of the hammer of the word which finally pulverizes the granite hardness of our rationalized hearts, making us yield to what God is saying to us. It is the truth, driven home by a heart made earnest in prayer, that melts, softens, and heals hearts, causing individuals to grow in grace and power. Only the word of God can teach a new Christian the difference between flashy, dedicated, zeal operating in the suave power of the flesh, and the quiet commitment of a Spirit-filled life which faithfully does a thing whether it is being observed or not.

Unfortunately, in American churches particularly, there has come a strange reversal of roles between the pastor and the evangelist. This has effectively deprived churches of the biblical ministry of a pastor and has resulted in a grossly impoverished and untaught people. Probably due to the influence of frontier living, the work of evangelism has been exalted over that of pastoral teaching in many American churches. Because in frontier America the evangelist was greatly admired and respected, pastors of frontier churches conceived of their role as that of an evangelist, whose task was to declare the initial truths of Christianity and win as many to Christ as possible. They began to evangelize in their pulpits, priding themselves on their faithfulness to their calling in proclaiming the gospel fearlessly, Sunday after Sunday. It became then the task of the people to bring others into the church to hear the pastor evangelize. But fewer and fewer came, and finally the pastor was left to evangelize the evangelized —week after week after week.

Since the saints were not led on into deeper and

clearer understanding of the great provisions of life and power available to them through the Spirit, they grew dull and bored with the gospel which they heard every week, and fell into apathy, criticism, quarreling, bickering, divisions and schisms, and eventually into dissolute living and the double standards of hypocrisy.

When this occurred, naturally the rate of conversions dropped off alarmingly and an evangelist was usually brought in to correct this. But he frequently found that the people were in no spiritual condition to undertake evangelism, and so he had to take a week or so of special meetings with the congregation and become a pastor to them, teaching them enough spiritual life that they could aid him in the subsequent outreach meetings. Thus the modern revivalist was born. The annual "revival" became the shot in the arm upon which most churches depended for any degree of advance or witness.

Naturally this picture is somewhat overdrawn, for the situation I have just described was not true everywhere, nor always to the same degree. There have always been strong churches where the pastor faithfully taught and applied the Scriptures and where Christians demonstrated a quality of life which made their communities sit up and take notice. Also, no one would wish to downgrade the splendid evangelism which has gone on for many decades in certain great preaching centers where thousands have found spiritual rebirth and, often, much helpful Bible teaching which has helped to make them into attractive and useful Christians. But as always, the good is the enemy of the best, and when the pastor becomes an evangelist and the evangelist is forced often to assume the role of a pastor, neither is performing his proper function within the body, and the whole body suffers greatly as a result.

There are, of course, men who have both the gifts of

an evangelist and a pastor. These are responsible to use both gifts in their ministries. But they should clearly understand that one gift is exercised toward Christians and the other toward non-Christians; one will be best performed in a meeting of Christians, while the other will take them outside the church to worldlings wherever they gather.

I have had the privilege of pastoring one church for over twenty-five years. In all that time we have never held an evangelistic meeting in the church, but there has been a continual stream of new converts coming into the church for instruction and development in the Christian life. Evangelism has been occurring within the homes of members, and in public halls, backyards, schoolrooms, and wherever a hearing for the gospel could be obtained. But every meeting held in the church building has been aimed at the instruction, training, or worship of Christians together. Our entire Sunday School is set up to equip the saints, of all ages, to do the work of the ministry. The work of expounding and applying the Scriptures begins with the pulpit and is continued in every class, in every gathering and in many of the homes of Christians. Stress is laid upon confronting life as it is really lived with the insights and viewpoints of Scripture and drawing upon the resurrection power of an ever-present Lord. Christians are taught to welcome contact with the world but to live distinctive lives in the midst of it, *sheep in the midst of wolves* as Jesus put it.

Certainly the primary responsibility for effective Christian training lies with those within the church who have the gift of pastor-teacher. As we have seen ideally this would include all the ruling elders, plus Sunday School teachers, young people's leaders, home Bible class teachers, small group leaders, etc., etc. They share together the responsibility of growing in the

93

knowledge of the word of God and of learning to impart it so as to instruct, admonish, rebuke, exhort, and encourage those who are under their care.

Little Tin Gods

Further, the Scriptures have much to say about the attitude of heart with which this pastoral work is done. If the term "shaping up the saints" conveys to you an image of an ecclesiastical top sergeant or a pastoral pop-off, who thunders denunciations at his people, then it is misleading. Pastors are not to be tyrants or bosses. Let's be honest and admit that there have been plenty around. Even in the early church there was at least one. His name was Diotrephes and you will find him mentioned in John's second letter where he called, *Diotrephes, who loves to have the preeminence.* But he is a far cry from the scriptural concept of a pastor.

The apostle Peter writes to certain pastors (or elders) as being himself *a fellow elder with you* and he exhorts them:

I urge you then to see that your "flock of God" is properly fed and cared for. Accept the responsibility of looking after them willingly and not because you feel you can't get out of it, doing your work not for what you can make, but because you are really concerned for their well-being. You should aim not at being "little tin gods" but as examples of Christian living in the eyes of the flock committed to your charge (1 Pet. 5:2,3, Phillips).

"Little tin gods" is a colorful modern expression for the Greek, "not as lords over God's heritage." The *RSV* renders it, *not as domineering over those in your charge.*

You can see that the Peter speaking here is quite different than the brash disciple of the Gospels. Here, chastened and humbled, he seeks to fulfill the commission the Lord Jesus gave him after the resurrection

94

when he thrice asked Peter, *Do you love me?* and thrice gave him the command, *Feed my Sheep.* Peter has now learned that the task of the shepherd is to feed the sheep, not to fleece them. He has learned to be a servant and not a lord over God's people.

These words are not to be taken lightly. Every pastor, especially, must heed these words. They must ever remember that they are not called to be bosses. They are but instruments, servants, examples. Once again, Jesus said, "When the good shepherd puts forth his sheep, he goes before them" (see John 10:4). That is, he does everything first. He leads his sheep by doing everything first. No teacher has the right to teach whose life does not exemplify his teaching. If he tries to say one thing and be another, the Chief Shepherd will suddenly pull the rug from under him and his ministry will be despised.

Again, the ministry of shepherding and teaching must be done without desiring personal glory. How well pastors know that right here is where the full force of temptation to pride can strike. There is something very pleasing to the ego to stand in front of others and have every eye fastened on you and every ear open to what you have to say. It is terribly easy to learn to love that feeling and to find subtle ways of nurturing and encouraging it.

As a pastor I must confess that I had to stop the practice of going to the door after a service and greeting people as they went out. I found that when I did it regularly it ministered to my ego in such a way that I had a terrible battle with pride. People were saying nice things to me and I found myself loving to hear them. It is very easy for a pastor or teacher to carry on his work for hidden reasons of personal prestige or glory. Pastors love to be regarded as dedicated, mature Christians. They are all too much aware, at times, of their seeming sacrifice of time and money to fulfill their calling. They can so easily think that they really deserve the attention and praise of others because they have been relatively faithful to what God has called them to do.

Of course, no pastor would ever say so publicly. But it is often evident in the hurt feelings they display when something doesn't go their way, or in their desire to quit if they haven't been noticed sufficiently. It is evident in the jealous cattiness which is sometimes displayed toward another's ministry, and in the sarcasm they use with their congregations, and in the false modesty they often display. I heard of a congregation which gave its pastor a medal for humility, but took it away again because he wore it!

To Get Attention

One further thing can be said about the ministry of equipping the saints through the exposition of the word of God. Paul describes his own ministry in these terms: *Him (Christ) we proclaim, warning every man and teaching every man in all wisdom, that we may present every man mature in Christ* (Col. 1:28). The process Paul followed in shaping up the saints was first to warn them and then to teach them. Teaching alone—the imparting of correct doctrine—is not enough. It must be preceded by the ministry of warning. Does it seem wrong to you (as it did to me) to put warning before teaching? Surely one teaches first, and then if the teaching is not received it is appropriate to warn of the results. But when I looked more closely at the original word translated "warning" I found that it is the Greek word for "mind" combined with the verb "to put." It means to put in mind or to call attention to something. It indicates that the first task of a teacher or pastor is to capture the attention and interest of his hearers.

96

There is a very old (perhaps even odorous) story about a man who wanted to train his mule. The first thing he did was to pick up a big stick and hit the mule a resounding wallop between the ears. As the mule staggered about someone asked the man, "Why did you do that?" And the man said, "In order to teach a mule anything you must get his full attention first." That is exactly what the apostle suggests is the proper order of teaching: interest must be first awakened, though certainly not as cruelly as the story of the mule suggests.

When Paul went to Athens to preach to the sophisticated Greeks he did not begin by mounting Mars Hill and saying, "Ladies and gentlemen of Athens, I have come to speak to you on the moral superiority of Christianity to paganism." That was the subject of his address but he did not begin in that way. He had been walking around the city noting certain things first, and when he got up to speak he said, "You people of Athens are certainly very religious. As I have gone about this city I have seen nothing but altars everywhere. I even found one erected to an Unknown God, which clearly indicates there is something about God which you don't yet know and that is what I have come to talk to you about." (From Acts 17:22-23.) Thus he had their attention, "putting them in mind" of what he wanted to announce. The key to true teaching is first to awaken interest and arouse attention.

One of the most amazing illustrations of the power of the ministry of equipping the saints is recorded in the nineteenth chapter of Acts. There Luke describes the ministry of Paul in the city of Ephesus, the very city to which Paul wrote later describing the ministry of the saints.

And he entered the synagogue and for three months spoke boldly, arguing and pleading about the kingdom of God; but when some were stubborn and disbelieved, speaking evil of the Way before the congregation, he withdrew from them, taking the disciples with him, and argued daily in the hall of Tyrannus. This continued for two years (Acts 19:8-10).

A marginal reading indicated that certain manuscripts add the words, *from the fifth hour to the tenth* after the sentence, *taking the disciples with him [he] argued daily in the hall of Tyrannus.* That would mean that Paul taught these new Christians for five hours a day, every day, for two years. That adds up to some 3650 hours of teaching. Is it any wonder that the tenth verse concludes . . . *so that all the residents of Asia heard the word of the Lord, both Jews and Greeks.* This means that within two years' time everyone who lived in the Roman province of Asia (of which Ephesus was the capital) was reached by the gospel. Not all believed, of course, but all heard. Who reached them? It was not the apostle Paul. He remained in Ephesus, teaching five hours a day. They were reached by a multitude of Christians, common ordinary "saints," who fanned out from Ephesus in the normal pursuit of their business and who exercised their spiritual gifts in such quiet power that the whole province was stirred by the amazing news of the gospel, and many responded to be themselves taught and empowered to carry the good news even further. That is the ministry of the saints.

CHAPTER NINE

The Work of the Ministry

Many are asking today, "Where is Jesus Christ at work in our world? How does he touch the problems of society in this twentieth century?" The answer is that he is at work exactly as he was at work in his lifetime on earth, doing precisely the same thing. In the days of his flesh he did his work through one solitary, earthly, physical body. He is doing the same work now through a corporate, complex body which exists around the world and permeates and penetrates every level of society. It is called, the church, the body of Christ, but its ministry is to the same race Jesus ministered to, under the same basic conditions, facing the same attitudes and problems.

We have seen that our Lord has endowed his corporate body with an array of spiritual gifts, capable of many combinations and designed to establish and improve relationships between any individual and God. He has also endued the members of his body with a new kind of power, resurrection power, which operates silently yet powerfully as a result of Christ's life within every believer. It is only when a Christian uses his spiritual gifts in resurrection power that his life becomes an extension of the incarnated life of Jesus. At all other times his activity is only that of the "natural" man without spiritual effect or power.

To Reach the World

In focusing on the gifts of the Spirit and the power in which they are operative we must not lose sight of the two-fold reason for the manifestation of these gifts. These are clearly stated as: (1) unto the work of the ministry and (2) unto the building up of the body of Christ. The gifts are given to be useful in these two realms, the world and the church. We must continually remember that the work of the ministry is to the world. The church exists as God's instrument to reach the world. *For God so loved the world that he gave his only Son* (John 3:16).

It is clearly God's intention that through the true church the world might see Jesus Christ at work. The world needs his ministry desperately, but it was never intended that worldlings should come to the church to find Christ. The church should be in the world. It is only thus that the world will understand that Christ is not dead, is not gone, and is not inactive. Jesus Christ is not off in some remote corner of the universe (heaven), nor has he left his people here to struggle on and do the best they can until he comes back again. This was never the divine intent nor is it the New Testa-

100

ment pattern. Christ is alive and has been at work in human society for twenty centuries, just as he said he would be: *Lo, I am with you always, to the close of the age* (Matt. 28:20).

Specifically, what is the ministry of the body of Christ? Let us hear the answer from his own lips. It is found in one of the most drama-filled scenes of the New Testament, recorded in the fourth chapter of Luke's Gospel. It is our Lord's own description of the ministry he came to accomplish on earth, whether in his physical body of flesh or in his corporate body (no less physical) of the church.

In verse 16 of chapter 4, Luke tells us:

And he came to Nazareth, where he had been brought up; and he went into the synagogue, as his custom was, on the sabbath day. And he stood up to read; and there was given to him the book of the prophet Isaiah.

Jesus began his ministry in the cities around the lake of Galilee with his headquarters in Capernaum. He then made an extensive journey into Jerusalem and Judea where he did many miracles. He soon gained a reputation throughout the land as a doer of good deeds and a worker of miracles. Word had come back to his hometown of Nazareth of the strange and remarkable things this local youth had been doing. Now he has returned and everyone in town knows that he will be in the synagogue on the sabbath day. They all turn out to hear him for they are anxiously hoping that he will do among them some of the miracles he has done in other cities. But in the synagogue he calls for the scroll of the prophet Isaiah, and unrolling it to the proper place (in our Old Testament, the sixty-first chapter of Isaiah) he read the following passage, as Luke reports it:

He opened the book and found the place where it was written, "The Spirit of the Lord is upon me, because he has anointed me to preach good news to the poor. He

has sent me to proclaim release to the captives and re-
covering of sight to the blind, to set at liberty those
who are oppressed, to proclaim the acceptable year of
the Lord." And he closed the book, and gave it back to
the attendant, and sat down; and the eyes of all in the
synagogue were fixed on him. And he began to say to
them, "*Today this scripture has been fulfilled in your*
hearing" (Luke 4:17-21).

There must have been many puzzled looks among
the townspeople of Nazareth at this point. They must
have said to themselves, "What does he mean? How
could he feel this Scripture was fulfilled among us when
he has done no miracles in Nazareth at all?" Knowing
this thought was in their hearts, Jesus went on to say to
them:

Doubtless you will quote to me this proverb, "Physi-
cian, heal yourself; what we have heard you did at Ca-
pernaum, do here also in your own country" (Luke
4:23).

Then he went on to remind them that in the history of
Israel it was often true that when a prophet came back
to his own country his people would not receive him.
He cited the two examples of Elijah and Elisha who
worked miracles of blessing for Gentiles but did not do
the same for any Israelites.

In what sense, therefore, did he mean that Isaiah's
great prophecy of the Messiah had been fulfilled in Nazareth? Doubtless he meant for them to see that the
physical fulfillment of these predictions (opening blind
eyes, healing the lame, etc.) was not the sole intent of
Scripture. The Messiah would indeed begin on that
level in order to capture attention and evoke trust in
himself, but he would also fulfill the predictions at a
deeper and more important level, that of the human
spirit. It is the healing of the hurt of the spirit in man
which God is really after, and it was on this level that

102

the prophecy of Isaiah had been fulfilled in Nazareth.

The Error of Israel

But the majority in Nazareth had their expectations
set on the physical alone. They wanted to see physical
miracles. They refused to accept his intimation that the
ultimate fulfillment was the healing of man's spirit.
They became exceedingly angry with him and organized a "lynch party," seeking to push him off the edge
of the precipice on which Nazareth was built.

It has been often pointed out that the miracles
which Jesus did are also parables, designed to teach on
the physical level what Christ offers to do on the
deeper level of the spirit. The mistake of the Jews during our Lord's ministry was that they would not accept
this but continually hounded him to give them an outward sign. Paul said it continued to be the desire of the
Jews even after the crucifixion and they would not
believe the gospel without some kind of sign (see 1
Cor. 1:22).

Those who hunger and thirst for physical miracles
today are repeating this error of Israel. They constantly
seek something visible, something obviously supernatural, something thrilling. As if a work done in the center
of a man's life is any less supernatural than something
done to the body. Jesus made it clear to the people of
Nazareth that the predicted ministry of the Messiah
had already been fulfilled in their midst by his presence among them.

With this in mind let us take this great word of
Isaiah's and look at it in closer detail, for it describes
not only the physical fulfillment which occurred in the
days of Jesus' presence in the flesh, but also the fulfillment which will occur through you as a Christian in
the twentieth century. Remember that Jesus said of his
disciples, *He who believes in me will also do the works*

that I do; and greater works than these will he do, because I go to the Father (John 14:12). What are these "greater works"? Anything done in the realm of the spirit is greater than that done in the body. All the bodily miracles which Jesus performed were but temporary cures, ending at the subsequent death of the individual involved. But whatever he did to the spirit of men in his day was eternal, yielding its blessing world without end.

When Jesus went to the Father he sent back the Holy Spirit who would reproduce the life of Jesus within the believer. Thus the church can do throughout the ages greater works than the Son of God did when he was here in the days of his flesh, for it is really not the church (or the individual Christian) doing them, but they are being done by a risen, ascended Lord through the Holy Spirit.

There are four divisions in this work of the ministry, introduced by the phrase, *The Spirit of the Lord is upon me because he has anointed me* (Luke 4:18). What follows is a description of a Spirit-filled ministry. As Jesus was anointed by the Spirit for his ministry in his lifetime, so each believer must be filled with the Spirit for the work he is to do. How can others tell when the Spirit of God is at work in any life? Will it be by the display of some strange phenomenon, or by a miraculous manifestation? No, the Spirit-filled ministry will be the kind of ministry described by Isaiah. It will open spiritually blinded eyes, make the spiritually lame walk, free those held spiritually captive, etc. That is the purpose of a Spirit-filled life.

First, the work of the ministry is to evangelize. *He has anointed me to preach good news to the poor* (Luke 4:18). The first division of the work of the ministry is that the saints (ordinary Christians) will declare the good news of God's historic actions among

104

men. That is evangelism. The good news is that God has not left the race to struggle on hopelessly in frustration, bewilderment, boredom, misery, and darkness. God has done something about it. He has acted to deliver men through his Son, Jesus Christ. God has himself gone to the cross and borne men's sins. He has acted and not merely spoken. Through the resurrection he has acted to give men his own life and thus empower them to live. To tell men this story is to preach the good news.

To whom is this to be preached? Well, not to the rich but to the poor! What does this mean? Surely it does not mean only those who are physically and materially poor. Are not the rich and the wealthy to hear this good news too? Obviously the prophecy goes beyond the physical again to the spiritual poverty of men. Remember the first words of the Sermon on the Mount, perhaps the greatest message ever delivered in the hearing of men? It begins with a remarkable recipe for happiness, the Beatitudes. *Blessed (happy) are the poor in spirit, for theirs is the kingdom of heaven.* That is, happy is the man who doesn't have any resources left in his spirit, and he knows it. Happy is the man who does not have any standing before God, who does not have a long record of good works to rest on and thus create a self-righteous attitude, but blessed is the man who comes to God and says, *Be merciful to me a sinner.* God is then able to give to that man the kingdom of heaven. Jesus never wasted much time with the self-righteous and the self-sufficient. He preached to the poor in spirit. Don't waste time talking to people who think they have everything they need. Look for those who have nothing, but don't be misled by the fact that some pretend to have everything while underneath there is a searching, hungry heart. Get down to that. Preach the good news to the poor.

Release and Recovery

The next assignment within the work of the ministry consists of two factors: *to proclaim release to the captives and recovering of sight to the blind* (Luke 4:18). Release and recovery of sight. Liberty and light. Do you know any captives, any people who are bound by outlooks and attitudes which hold them in perpetual captivity? Do you know anyone who is struggling to free himself from hurtful habits which hold him in a vise-like grip and which defeat every effort he makes to be free? Do you know any who are locked into a pattern of poisonous hate, or jealous bitterness, or possessive greed which they seem powerless to break? Are you such a one yourself? Then there is good news! Jesus Christ is able to free. He has done it for millions and he can do it for you.

Are there people who are blind today? Are there men and women who think they are doing the right thing and who mean to do the right thing but somehow it always turns out wrong? They are blind, they cannot see to the end of the paths they are on. Often they are perfectly sincere, honest people, who hope they are doing right and are struggling the best they can, but nothing works out and they end up stumbling blindly from one episode to another, deeper and deeper into difficulty. Are not these people blind? They are in need of a ministry which proclaims the recovering of sight to the blind.

This releasing and recovering ministry is the result of teaching the truth. Jesus said, *You will know the truth, and the truth will make you free* (John 8:32). That is what releases captives and recovers sight: telling men the truth. Not telling men what they want to hear but telling them what they need to hear. Jesus said, *He who follows me will not walk in darkness, but will have the light of life* (John 8:12). That is also the work of teaching: to disciple men, to show them how to follow Jesus. Not merely to come to church and sing about Jesus, or to recite a creed, but to obey him, even when every fiber of their being is crying out to disobey him. Obviously this work of teaching touches what we are doing every day of our lives. It involves us at our work, in our home, at school, at shop, at play, when we are awake, wherever we are. Part of the work of the ministry is to teach men and women, boys and girls, how to lay hold of the power that releases from captivity, and to follow and obey the one who opens eyes so that no man need walk in darkness.

A Demonic Element

The next element of a Spirit-filled ministry is *to set at liberty those who are oppressed* (Luke 4:18). At first glance this seems similar to proclaiming release to captives. It is true that the end result is the same: liberty. But the problem of oppression is a much deeper and more serious one than mere captivity. Oppression has a demonic element about it. It is more than mere tyranny, there is also a terrible cruelty involved. It results in a sense of burden, of dejection and depression, coupled with hopelessness.

Once a man drove over 600 miles to tell me of a heavy burden which was oppressing him. For over a year he had been terribly affected by an attitude of hate toward a man who had done him a great injustice. He could not free himself of his bitterness and rancor. It began to trouble him so that he could not eat or sleep properly. On two or three occasions he had barely been able to restrain himself from committing murder. It was breaking him up and destroying his family and threatening his own life. He was troubled by constant depression and despair.

107

We talked together and I showed him the truth of the Scripture about his unforgiving spirit. Gently I explained to him that he was poisoning his own life by his hatred and there could be no release till he was able to forgive the man who had offended him. He agreed to ask God for the grace to do so, and we prayed together. As we prayed I watched his face and before my eyes a miracle took place. I saw a man healed, a burden lifted, the oppressed freed. I watched the poison of hate drain out of that man's heart and the love of Jesus Christ come flooding in. His whole attitude visibly changed. Soon he went home with a different look on his face and a different attitude in his heart.

Such is the ministry of counseling and prayer which gives liberty to the oppressed. It doesn't take a pastor to do it, but can be done by any Christian who knows the truth of the word and has faith to pray. This man should not have had to drive 600 miles to find someone to help him. But unfortunately this ministry of prayer-counseling has been left for the professional counsellor to handle and problems which could have been easily handled when small have grown into terribly tangled knots which even professionals cannot always handle. Prayer is particularly effective in problems of this type. Jesus once said of a demon-ridden boy, *This kind cannot be driven out by anything but prayer* (Mark 9:29).

The last element of the work of Christ's body in the world today is: *to proclaim the acceptable year of the Lord* (Luke 4:19). This is one of the most remarkable statements in the Bible. If you will look up the original passage in Isaiah from which Jesus read, you will discover that there is a comma after the word "Lord." The sentence is not complete at that point. In the original it goes on to say: *and to declare the day of vengeance of our God* (Isa. 61:1,2). The Lord Jesus did not read that

108

part of the script. At the comma he closed the book and handed it back saying, *Today this scripture has been fulfilled in your hearing* (Luke 4:21). He thereby implied that at that point in time the rest was not yet fulfilled. *The day of vengeance of our God* awaits the second return of Jesus Christ. But the present age is *the acceptable year of the Lord*. Salvation is still possible.

To proclaim this great fact is to explain what is happening in our world. It is to relieve the cold grip of fear which clutches at the hearts of thousands who get up every morning scared to death, not knowing what will happen to a world that has apparently gone quite mad. They are afraid that history is out of control. They fear that God has lost command over human events, if he ever had it. They feel lost, helpless, victims of inexorable forces far beyond men.

They need someone to proclaim to them the acceptable year of the Lord. They need to see from the Scriptures that God knows what he is doing in our day and age, that he is restraining the forces of evil to permit the gospel to go out, but permitting sufficient demonstration of the evil in man that they may see it themselves and recognize their desperate need. God is governing human events according to his own purposes and on his own timetable. The acceptable year of the Lord will go on only as long as God decrees, but till it ends no man can go beyond God's limits of restraint.

There is the work of the ministry: evangelizing, teaching, praying, explaining the times. That is the task of the church in the world. Is it relevant? Is it something people need, something they are dying for, are desperate to find? I will leave that for you to answer, but if you see it as I do you will recognize that nothing could be more exciting and fulfilling than to be involved in ministry like this. If you are a Christian this is your ministry. To this end you have been equipped by being given certain spiritual gifts, and it is for this purpose that you have within you the power of a risen Lord from which to draw. The pastor and evangelist, along with the apostles and prophets, are there only to help you with this ministry. They cannot do it themselves. They exist to help you, not you to help them.

A Normal Part of Life

Perhaps you say, "But when can I do this? After all, I have to earn a living and don't have time to go about preaching and teaching." There is an easy answer to that. Do it at work. Do it in your home. This ministry is as natural and normal a part of life as anything else you can do. Obviously, the majority of Christians spend their time doing the work of the world, and this is as it should be. Not everyone is called to be a pastor or an evangelist, or even a teacher. The major preoccupation of any man's life is his daily employment. But if Jesus Christ has no part in that then he is Lord only of the margins of your life, of the spare time, the leftovers.

Have you ever noticed that the really important figures of the New Testament are not the priests and monks. They are shepherds, fishermen, taxgatherers, soldiers, politicians, tentmakers, physicians, and carpenters. These are the ones who occupy the center of the stage. So it must be again today. You can tell the good news of God at work around a water cooler in an office if the occasion is right. Or to another, over a lunch bucket. You can heal a hurt heart in a car while you are driving home. You can teach the truth that frees over a cup of coffee in a kitchen, or pray the prayer of deliverance beside a sick bed. You can interject Christian insights into business transactions or governmental problems and they may mean the difference between conflict and strife, between heaven and hell.

A Christian man told me recently that he is a member of an urban renewal committee in San Francisco, responsible for clearing up certain slum areas in that city. At one of their meetings the board was contemplating setting up a new housing project in an area already crowded with tenements and flats. They faced the question of what to do about the people who would be displaced until the new housing was ready. There was a general feeling of "That's their problem, let them take care of it." But this man said, "No, it is not their problem, it's our problem. We have no right to put in a housing project unless we face the responsibility of helping these people find some other place to live. Christian compassion can do nothing less!" He stood his ground and because he spoke up at a critical moment he made the committee face their responsibility and they eventually found a way to solve it.

In these apocalyptic times it is easy to find an occasion to proclaim the acceptable year of the Lord. It is almost impossible to avoid it! You can quiet the fearful with a reassuring word of hope in almost any situation. All you need is a newspaper headline or a television commentary and you have a wide open door to tell men of what God is doing in history and where he says it will all end.

We must never forget our Lord's story of the sheep and the goats, and the basis of their judgment. The whole point of the story is that Christians must not evade activities that involve them in the hurt of the world. The hungry must be fed, the naked clothed, the sick visited, and those in prison encouraged. We must put our gifts to work. We dare not hide them in the ground as that unfaithful steward did in one of the Lord's parables, for we must someday meet him for an accounting.

CHAPTER TEN

Keeping the Body Healthy

The work of the ministry, as we have seen, is directed toward a suffering and desperate world. It requires every member of the body of Christ to accomplish it effectively, as God intended it to be done. It also requires that the members of the body shall be spiritually healthy, vibrant with the life of Christ who indwells them through his Spirit.

No athlete spends all his time running races or playing the game for which he is trained; he must also spend many hours keeping himself in shape and developing his skills to a high degree. So it is also with the body of Christ. The work of the ministry will never be properly done by a weak and unhealthy church, torn with internal pains, and wracked by spiritual diseases. Thus it is no surprise that the pattern of the Holy Spirit for the operation of Christ's body should indicate that apostles, prophets, evangelists, and pastor-teachers exist not only to equip the saints to the work of the ministry, but also to aid and support them in a mutual ministry to each other which results in *building up the body of Christ*.

Unhealthy Saints

Great damage has been done by unhealthy saints attempting to reach out to the world in evangelism or social help in spasms of dedicated zeal, but without true spiritual health. Burdened with unsolved problems in their own lives, and unconsciously displaying unresolved hypocrisies of prejudice and outlook, their spasmodic activities in evangelism or help seem to be but hollow mockeries of Christianity in the eyes of those they hope to reach. Their own Christian meetings have turned into dull, stodgy rituals where many Christians gather to go through completely predictable performances, all conducted in an atmosphere of "reverence" which permits no interchange with one another, no exchange of thought, no discussion of truth, and no opportunity to display Christian love in any but the most superficial of ways.

What is terribly missing is the experience of "body life"; that warm fellowship of Christian with Christian which the New Testament calls *koinonia*, and which was an essential part of early Christianity. The New Testament lays heavy emphasis upon the need for Christians to know each other, closely and intimately enough to be able to bear one another's burdens, confess faults one to another, rebuke, exhort, and admonish one another, minister to one another with the word and through song and prayer, and thus come to comprehend *with all saints* as Paul puts it, *what is the breadth and length and height and depth, and to know the love of Christ which surpasses knowledge* (Eph. 3:18,19).

Where, in the usual, traditional, church structure of meetings is this kind of interchange possible? What provision is made by church leaders to encourage it and guide its expression through scriptural teaching and wise admonitions? Some expression of it has occurred in private gatherings of Christians, usually in someone's home, but all too often this has been discouraged by church leaders as "divisive," or at least viewed as a threat to the unity of the church.

But in the early church a kind of rhythm of life was evident in which the Christians would gather together in homes to instruct one another, study and pray together, and share the ministry of spiritual gifts. Then they would go out into the world again to let the warmth and glow of their love-filled lives overflow into a spontaneous Christian witness that drew love-starved pagans like a candy store draws little children. This was exactly in line with the exhortation of Jesus to his disciples:

A new commandment I give to you, that you love one another; even as I have loved you, that you also love one another. By this all men will know that you are my disciples, if you have love for one another (John 13:34, 35).

The early church thus relied upon a two-fold witness as the means of reaching and impressing a cynical and unbelieving world: *kerygma* (proclamation) and *koinonia* (fellowship). It was the combination of these two which made their witness so powerful and effective. "In the mouth of two or three witnesses shall every word be established" (see Matt. 18:16). Pagans could easily

114

shrug off the proclamation as simply another "teaching" among many; but they found it much more difficult to reject the evidence of *koinonia.* The concern of Christians for each other and their evident awareness of sharing life in the same great family of God as brothers and sister, left the pagan world drooling with envy. It prompted the much-quoted remark of a pagan writer: "How these Christians love one another!"

The present-day church has managed to do away with *koinonia* almost completely, reducing the witness of the church to proclamation (*kerygma*) alone. It has thus succeeded in doing two things simultaneously: removing the major safeguard to the health of the church from within, and greatly weakening its effective witness before the world without. It is little wonder, therefore, that the church has fallen on evil days and is regarded as irrelevant and useless by so many in the world.

Fulfilling Christ's Law

It is time to take seriously again certain admonitions of Scripture which have somehow been passed over lightly even by so-called Bible-believing Christians. Take, for instance, this strong word from Galatians 6:2: *Bear one another's burdens, and so fulfill the law of Christ.* Note that the apostle indicates that this is the way by which the fundamental law of the Christian life is fulfilled. That law is the word of Jesus, quoted above: *A new commandment I give to you, . . . that you also love one another* (John 13:34). The law of love is fulfilled only by bearing one another's burdens. But how can Christians bear each other's burdens if they don't know what they are? Some way of sharing these burdens with others is obviously called for. It calls for honesty and openness with other Christians, and a mutual recognition that it is neither abnormal nor unspiritual to have burdens and problems in one's Christian experience. Somehow the masks have to come off and facades that say "everything-is-all-right" when everything is anything but right, have to be removed. Often this can be done best in small groups, meeting in homes, though it may surprise many to discover how much larger meetings of Christians can be characterized by such a spirit of loving, non-judgmental acceptance, that many deeply personal problems can be shared openly without fear of rejection or giving rise to scandal. (Chapter twelve will describe just such a meeting which often involves over a thousand people.)

Bearing one another's burdens at the very least means to uphold one another in prayer. It also means to be willing to spend time with another person in thoroughly understanding his problem, and committing oneself to certain effort to relieve pressure or discouragement, or in finding some way to help financially or by wise counsel. Christians must not transfer such responsibility to governmental authorities, either national or local. Help available from such sources should be welcomed and used, but nothing can take the place of an arm around the shoulder, a repeated time of prayer together, or a steadying word of counsel from a brother or sister in the family of God.

Another direct exhortation from the word is that of James 5:16: *Confess your sins one to another, and pray for one another, that you may be healed.* Confessing faults certainly means to admit weaknesses and to acknowledge failures in living as Christians. It is often difficult to get Christians to do this, despite the clear directive of the word. It goes against the grain to give an image of oneself that is anything less than perfect, and many Christians imagine that they will be rejected by others if they admit to any faults. But nothing could be more destructive to Christian *koinonia* than the

116

common practice today of pretending not to have any problems. It is often true that Christian homes may be filled with bickering, squabbling, angry tantrums, even bodily attacks of one member of the family against another, and yet not one word of this is breathed to anyone else and the impression is carefully cultivated before other Christians that this is an ideal Christian family with no problems of any serious consequence to be worked out.

To make matters even worse, this kind of conspiracy of silence is regarded as the Christian thing to do, and the hypocrisy it presents to other (not to mention how it appears to individual members of the family) is considered to be part of the family's "witness" to the world. How helpful, how wonderfully helpful, it would be if one of the members of this family (preferably the father) would honestly admit in a gathering of fellow Christians that his family was going through difficulties in working out relationships with one another, and needed very much their prayers and counsel through this time of struggle. The family member would immediately discover at least two things: (1) that every other Christian in the meeting identified with his problem and held him in higher esteem than ever because of his honesty and forthrightness; and (2) a wealth of helpful counsel would be opened to him from those who had gone through similar struggles and had learned very valuable lessons thereby. Further, the prayers of other Christians willing to help him bear his burden would release great spiritual power into the situation so that members of the family would be able to see much more clearly the issues to be resolved and be empowered to bear with patience and love the weaknesses of each other. The very next verse in the book of James, following the injunction to confess faults is: *The prayer of a righteous man has great power in its effects.*

Restoration of Koinonia

It is most significant that whenever spiritual awakenings have occurred throughout the Christian centuries they have always been accompanied by a restoration of *koinonia*, of the confession of faults, and the bearing of one another's burdens. During the Wesleyan awakening in eighteenth century England, the great evangelist George Whitefield wrote to his converts:

"My brethren . . . let us plainly and freely tell one another what God has done for our souls. To this end you would do well, as others have done, to form yourselves into little companies of four or five each, and meet once a week to tell each other what is in your hearts; that you may then also pray for and comfort each other as need shall require. None but those who have experienced it can tell the unspeakable advantages of such a union and communion of souls. . . . None I think that truly loves his own soul and his brethren as himself, will be shy of opening his heart, in order to have their advice, reproof, admonition and prayers, as occasions require. A sincere person will esteem it one of the greatest blessings."[1]

When this kind of sharing and burden bearing is occurring in a church it will go far in relieving the load of counselling that elders or pastors must do. Many emotional and even mental problems would be solved at their beginnings through the genuine love and concern of other Christians and would never grow into the complicated tangles that now require long hours of skilled counselling to unravel. Modern techniques of group therapy are built on this same basic principle of a common sharing that the early church so richly enjoyed.

1. Quoted by John R.W. Stott in *One People: Laymen & Clergy in God's Church* (Downers Grove, Ill.: Inter-Varsity Press paperback), p. 88.

Obviously there are certain intimate or scandalous matters that should not be voiced in an open meeting. Some types of sharing should be done privately between only two or three individuals who are trustworthy and mature in their insights. But no Christian should bear a heavy burden alone. Those with the gift of encouragement should make themselves available to others for this ministry, and any who appear to be withdrawn or downcast should be gently encouraged to unload. The gift of a listening ear and an understanding heart is sometimes the greatest gift one Christian can give another. Essential to this matter of building up or edifying the body of Christ is the apostle's admonition in Ephesians 4:15: *speaking the truth in love.* In the Greek it is simply "truthing in love." It has in its meaning not only speaking the truth but demonstrating it in every area of life.

Unloving Silence

Once again the common practice of Christians toward each other fails greatly at this point. We all tend to shy away from an unpleasant confrontation. If someone has an unpleasant or irritating habit or manner we are willing enough to talk about it to others, but seldom say anything to the person directly. If we do, it is usually only when we have been angered or irritated to the point of sharp and caustic protest. Our reason for silence is most often that "we don't wish to hurt him." That, of course, is self-deception. It is ourselves that we don't wish to hurt by having to tell someone a painful truth. In actual fact we do the other person incalculable harm by our unloving silence, for we condemn him or her to go on offending others and suffering rejection without realizing what it is that is creating the problem. No one loves him enough to take him aside and lovingly and understandingly point out the offending

119

practice. The worst thing of all is to baptize the silence and think of it as a mark of Christian love.

Yet every Christian has had occasion to be grateful beyond words for the loving admonition of some friend or brother who has helped him to see a blind spot and showed him how to lay hold of the grace of God to overcome an annoying and disagreeable habit. *Faithful are the wounds of a friend* (Prov. 27:6). We must again take most seriously the words of Galatians 6:1: *Brethren, if a man is overtaken in any trespass, you who are spiritual should restore him in a spirit of gentleness. Look to yourself, lest you too be tempted.*

This is the ministry of washing one another's feet which Jesus said was most necessary among his disciples: *If I then, your Lord and Teacher, have washed your feet, you also ought to wash one another's feet. For I have given you an example, that you also should do as I have done to you* (John 13:14,15). That he meant this to be taken symbolically and not literally is seen in his words, *What I am doing you do not know now, but afterward you will understand* (John 13:7). One can never do this work of washing another's feet without taking the place of a servant as our Lord did. But, as Dr. H. A. Ironside used to say, it helps greatly to be careful of the temperature of the water we use! Some come to others with icy, cold water and say "Here, stick your feet in here." Their cold, forbidding attitude arouses only resentment. Others are so angry and upset themselves when they come that it is like offering to wash another's feet in boiling water. The only way is to come with warm water which makes the unpleasant task of footwashing as pleasurable as possible. The one thing we must not do is to turn away and leave the offending person unrestored and unhelped.

A healthy body is necessary to do effective work. To attempt evangelism while the body of Christ is sick and ailing is worse than useless. It is not difficult to keep a body of Christians healthy and vital if the individuals involved (especially leaders) are concerned to bear one another's burdens, confess their faults one to another, and to instruct and admonish one another in love, by means of the word of God. It is by these means that the church is becoming what its Lord desires: *a church . . . in splendor, without spot or wrinkle or any such thing* (Eph. 5:27).

CHAPTER ELEVEN

The Goal Is Maturity

We must now look together at Paul's great statement
of the end and goal of all God's great far-flung enterprise among men. What is God doing through the
church? What is he after? What is the end of it all?
Paul says it is,

. . . *until we all attain to the unity of the faith and of
the knowledge of the Son of God, to mature manhood,
to the measure of the stature of the fullness of Christ; so
that we may no longer be children, tossed to and fro
and carried about with every wind of doctrine, by the
cunning of men, by their craftiness in deceitful wiles.
Rather, speaking the truth in love, we are to grow up
in every way into him who is the head, into Christ,*

from whom the whole body, joined and knit together by every joint with which it is supplied, when each part is working properly, makes bodily growth and up-builds itself in love (Eph. 4:13-16).

Twice in this great passage the apostle gives us the ultimate goal of the life of faith. It is the measuring stick by which we can judge our progress as Christians. In verse 13 he says it is *the measure of the stature of the fullness of Christ.* And in verse 15 he urges us *to grow up in every way into him who is the head, into Christ.* He puts it also in a most descriptive phrase, "mature manhood"! That means you and I, fulfilling our humanity, being what God had in mind when he made man and woman in the first place.

Note that the supreme purpose of the church is not the evangelization of the world. I know that is often held up to us as the supreme aim and purpose of the church. Certainly there is a great commission in the Bible and Jesus has sent us out to preach the gospel to every creature. This is a most important thing, but it is not the supreme thing, not the final goal. Romans 8:29 speaks of God predestinating his own *to be conformed to the image of his Son.* That is the ultimate end of all evangelization.

Nor does Paul say anything here about accomplishing world peace and universal justice. He does not say the church will ultimately introduce the millennium. We may well believe in the great vision of the prophets that there is coming a day when peace shall reign on the earth and men shall melt their spears into pruning hooks and their swords into plowshares and make war no more. One day righteousness shall prevail over all the earth and all the stories of injustice, heartache, tragedy, and hate with which we are so familiar today will be forgotten. But that is not the great and final purpose for the existence of the church.

The supreme thing, the paramount thing, the thing God is after above everything else is to produce in this present world men and women who are like the humanity of Jesus Christ. He does not want white-robed saints, or accomplished churchmen, or religious experts; what he wants is that you and I may be grown up, responsible, well-adjusted, wholehearted, human beings like Jesus Christ!

Our Heart's Desire

Deep in your own heart, is that not what you yourself passionately desire? You want to be a whole person, a complete human being. You want to discover and fulfill all that God has built into you. The proof that this is deep in every human heart is a fact which psychologists confirm—we all have a mental image of ourselves which approaches, in some considerable degree, our ideal of humanity. We tend to think of ourselves as much more mature than we really are. Our power of self-deceit is often almost incredible. Even in those times when we are trying to be ruthless and brutally honest about ourselves we can detect a self-esteem that is frightening. We may say, "I'm a stubborn, foolish, selfish person," but let someone agree with us at that point and we immediately bristle and say, "What do you mean? Why do you say that?" It is all because we long so to fulfill our humanity, to be the kind of persons we would like to be.

But that is what the church is all about. It is the vehicle designed by God to achieve mature humanity—a humanity exactly like Jesus Christ. We have now come full circle for this is where the apostle began: the church is to fulfill its calling which is that of demonstrating in the world a new character (lowliness, love, and unity) through a body which is inhabited by God himself.

As I think about the subject of spiritual maturity, I find that I need right away to define and distinguish between two words that are used frequently today: *spirituality* and *maturity*. It seems to me that the spiritual life is to a considerable degree an analogy of the physical life of an individual. If so, then I would view spirituality as the counterpart to physical health. Spirituality is simply spirtual good health. It involves keeping the mind and the will centered on the revelations of God and on the viewpoint of God about life, resulting in a habit of spiritual thinking which *expects* God to work in and through the doing of normal human activities.

Now, I grant that no one does this very well at first. Spirituality is a condition of openness to the Spirit of God as well as responsiveness to the will of God as it is made clear to us. In a person's early life as a Christian, he obviously does not understand a great deal about the will of God; much of the revealed truth of the word is hidden from him. Even though he is able to read it in the Bible, he doesn't really understand it. He needs spirituality right from the beginning, therefore, to enable him to grow in the ability to appropriate the knowledge of the word, just as a boy or a girl needs bodily health to move from infancy to adulthood. If a child's health fades, then his maturity is threatened but healthy children will inevitably keep on maturing. So also in the spiritual realm, if spirituality—the habit of spiritual thinking—is a condition of life, then maturity will be the result.

A Relative Concept

Having defined spirituality in those terms, I see *maturity* as the full range of understanding of the knowledge and will of God, increasing in depth as one grows older. It includes the entire range of experience to which a

125

Christian can be subjected. If you think of it this way, you can see immediately that maturity must be considered as a relative concept. We can say that someone is more or less mature than someone else but we cannot say that he has arrived at an objective standard by which he can be described as a fully mature person. When we do use the term in an objective sense, we are unconsciously using a certain gradient, such as "the usual run of persons" or "the average Christian" or some such thing. With this sort of unspoken comparison, we are able to say that certain people are mature.

The apostle Paul uses this term "mature," or as it is sometimes translated in the Scriptures "perfect," in both a relative and an absolute sense. In Philippians 3:12 for instance, he says, *Not that I have already obtained this or am already perfect.* There he announces that he realizes he has not reached perfection which, of course, only Jesus Christ himself ever manifested. But in the same passage, the apostle says in verse 15, *Let those of us who are mature* (or perfect) *be thus minded.* Here he speaks of himself, as well as others around him, as being mature. This is obviously the relative use of the term and means a greater maturity than is usually found in the church.

The apostle John in his first letter has given us a helpful way to gauge various levels of maturity. In 1 John 2:12 the apostle says, *I am writing to you, little children, because your sins are forgiven for his sake. I am writing to you, fathers, because you know him who is from the beginning. I am writing to you, young men, because you have overcome the evil one.*

When he speaks of certain Christians as *little children* the thing that characterizes them is that they know their sins are forgiven. Certainly that is the first thing a new Christian learns. Therefore, as long as they are reveling (and quite properly) in that stage of understanding, glorying in the fact that their sins are for-given—as long as they are rejoicing in the forgiveness of sin as the central thing about the Christian faith—they can be classified as little children. Now, John doesn't mean, of course, that they are to forsake that as they go on, because they will have a continually increasing awareness of the greatness of forgiveness of sin as they go through life. He simply means that a focus on forgiveness marks the initial stage of the Christian life.

Then he says, *I am writing to you, fathers, because you know him who is from the beginning.* For a long time I thought John was referring to God the Father, the one who is from the beginning. But thinking back to the way he opens the letter I began to realize that this is really a reference to the Son: *That which was from the beginning, which we have heard, which we have seen with our eyes, which we have looked upon and touched with our hands, concerning the word of life.* Here he is obviously referring to the Lord Jesus himself. The mark of being a *father* then, is a deep and thorough understanding of the deity and the humanity of Jesus, the fullness of the revelation that has come to us through the Son. It is to have a deep sense of acquaintanceship with him, of closeness to him, of having walked with him through much of life. Out of that closeness comes a clarity of understanding of Jesus' words to such a degree that there is a grasp of the great doctrines which he came to reveal. This level of maturity means to display an understanding and a manifestation of the same character which Jesus consistently manifested, and a compassion and a tolerance and a patience which only long-term association with the Son of God can produce. This is the mark of a father.

Finally, the *young men* are characterized as having overcome the evil one, as having reached a stage of maturity where there is an understanding and a practice of the way to resist temptation. Temptation, of course, comes from the evil one and the ability to handle temptation is a mark of a maturing individual, one who knows how to distinguish between good and evil. As the writer of Hebrews puts it, *But solid food is for the mature, for those who have their faculties trained by practice to distinguish good from evil* (Heb. 5:14). The kind of person who is overcoming the wicked one is able to see evil as evil even when it looks good, by the revelation of the Scriptures and by the understanding given by the Spirit. This is the mark of a young man.

Amplified Version

Now the apostle goes on to repeat these three, adding one or two things to amplify his thought. He says, *I write to you, children, because you know the Father.* That, of course, is how they came to forgiveness of sin. They came into an awareness of the fatherhood of God by faith in Jesus Christ, when God immediately became a father to them. The two things that mark the beginning experience of a Christian, then, are that wonderful sense of sins having been forgiven and of belonging to a family under God the Father. Then he says again, *I write to you, fathers, because you know him who was from the beginning.* No change there; it simply cannot be improved upon. The mark of a mature individual is to know Jesus Christ, growing continually in an understanding of his teachings—both directly and through his apostles—and to be able to live for long periods of time by the Spirit in reproducing the character of Jesus.

Now he says, *I write to you, young men, because you are strong, and the word of God abides in you, and you have overcome the evil one.* There he gives us a little further insight into how the *young men* overcome the evil one. They are strong—strong in spirit, that is—and they are responsive to what they're learning. Furthermore, the word of God abides in them; it is the truth they are learning that makes them strong. They are functional, able to be useful in the kingdom of God. This passage in John's letter illuminates the process of *growth;* maturity does not happen all at once. Returning to Ephesians 4, in verse 15 Paul says, *We are to grow up in every way . . . into Christ.* Then again, in the latter part of verse 16, he says the body *makes bodily growth and upbuilds itself in love.* Growth is God's method. It is a process, and it does not happen overnight. It is a matter that requires time.

I would like to suggest that that is very important. I know many Christians who are greatly disturbed when, having become Christians, they do not find themselves suddenly and remarkably transformed into angelic creatures. They still find much of the old life very much present. The old attitudes are still gripping and controlling their lives. They do not know what to make of this and many are tempted to believe that it is a sign they are not true Christians at all. If their faith is in Christ of course they are Christians, but they need to learn that there is a process of growth which must follow and it requires some time for growth to occur.

This necessity for growth is why the Scriptures warn against putting someone into a position of authority who is a novice, a new Christian. He simply has not had enough experience to have matured him to the place of carrying responsibility. The growth of his intellectual knowledge of Christian doctrine may have been most rapid and impressive, but knowledge alone does not make a man of God. Time alone is no guarantee of growth, but if the factors that make for growth are present it still requires some time before adequate growth can occur.

How Do You Grow?

New Christians should also understand that growth does not come by trying. You cannot, as Jesus pointed out, by taking thought add a cubit to your stature. You cannot say, "Now I am going to try to grow." Children would grow much faster than they do if that would work, but it does not. Well then, how do you grow? You must make sure that the factors that make for growth are present. If they are, growth will occur of itself, naturally and unforced. We have already examined many of these factors, but they are summarized by the apostle in this last passage as twofold: increasing in *the unity of the faith* and in *the knowledge of the Son of God*. These, he says, will lead to mature manhood, *the measure of the stature of the fullness of Christ* (Eph. 4:13).

The *unity of the faith* is the shared understanding, in the church, of the great truths revealed in the Scriptures. New light is continually issuing forth from the Scriptures through individual prophets and teachers who are given these new insights by the Holy Spirit. But then they must be shared widely in the body or no new truth is given. New Christians grow when they exert themselves to understand the Scriptures with the help of the teachers and leaders who make themselves available to them within the body of Christ. No growth into wholeness can occur without this increase in the unity of the faith through the understanding of Christian doctrine.

But it must also be accompanied by an increase in *the knowledge of the Son of God*. This refers to experience, to a growing encounter with the Lord Jesus himself, so that one comes to know him more and more, directly and personally. That, too, is necessary for maturity. It is the other factor that makes growth possible.

This encounter occurs when the knowledge of the faith is put into practice. You cannot know Jesus Christ until you follow him. The disciples had an acquaintance with Jesus Christ before they became his disciples. That is obvious from the gospel records. But they never knew him until they left everything and followed him. It is here that we are particularly helped by the prayers and concern of the other members of the body. In our relationships with one another our experience of the Lord who lives within us is deepened and enlarged. *Inasmuch as ye have done it unto one of the least of these my brethren, ye have done it unto me* (Matt. 25:40, *KJV*). So Jesus said when he revealed the standard of judgment for the last day.

Since growth is a matter of knowledge plus obedience plus time, we do not need to be discouraged if we find that we are not yet completely like Christ. One of the popular buttons circulating among Christians has the letters P B P G I N T W M Y printed on it. They stand for, "Please Be Patient, God Is Not Through With Me Yet." That great fact must never be used to defend an unwillingness to change, for the proper state of a healthy Christian is an eagerness to grow. I remember asking a boy once how old he was. Quick as a flash he said, "I'm twelve, going on thirteen, soon be fourteen." We do not need to ask ourselves, "Am I mature? Am I completely like Christ?" What we need to ask is, "Am I on the way? Is there progress? Am I growing in the right direction?"

No Longer Children

To help us in this evaluation the apostle gives us two practical means by which we can measure our growth toward full maturity. One is negative and the other is positive. He puts it negatively first:

So that we may no longer be children, tossed to and

fro and carried about with every wind of doctrine, by the cunning of men, by their craftiness in deceitful wiles (Eph. 4:14).

If you wish to know whether you are growing or not, do not measure yourself by comparison with someone else. That will tell you nothing. But ask yourself, "Am I moving away from childish attitudes? Am I forsaking infantile behavior? Am I still governed by childish reactions and outbursts?" That is the first way to measure your degree of maturity.

It is important to note that the Scriptures often exhort us to be childlike, but never to be childish. Those are two quite different things. Childlikeness is that refreshing simplicity of faith which believes God and acts without questioning. But childishness is described here by the apostle as instability and naïveté.

Children are notoriously fickle. Their attention span is not very long. You cannot interest them in one thing without their soon losing interest and turning to something else. They are unstable, tossed to and fro, and carried about by every changing circumstance. This is the invariable mark of an immature believer in Christ, whether he be new in the faith or undeveloped in his Christian experience. There are fads and fashions in the religious life and immature Christians are forever riding the crest of a new fad. They are always running after the newest book or teacher and extolling them as though they were the ultimate answer to spiritual need. I have come to recognize through the years that this is a mark of immaturity. They do not talk about the Bible that way, yet the Bible is the most exciting book of all.

This vacillation can be seen in the realm of actions as well. The childish Christian manifests himself by unfaithfulness, undependability. Many times new Christians will undertake some ministry or task with great eagerness and interest. But it is not very long before their interest wanes and they run out of gas and become discouraged. Soon they do not show up at all. This unreliability can easily be forgiven in new Christians but when it is manifested by those who have been Christians for many years it is much harder to bear. But part of the fruit of the Spirit is faithfulness—*love, joy, peace, patience, kindness, goodness, faithfulness, gentleness, self-control* (Gal. 5:22,23).

A second mark of childishness is to be undiscerning, naïve. Have you ever noticed how children are often unaware of danger? They may play in dangerous situations and be quite unaware that anything is threatening them. Thus young Christians are often caught by *the cunning of men, by their craftiness in deceitful wiles* (Eph. 4:14). This is an apt description of the many cultists, religious racketeers, charlatans, false prophets and teachers, who abound in our day and who trap many young Christian (and older, immature, believers as well) in their innocent sounding teachings. A childish attitude is always manifest by a confident assurance, an arrogant certainty that no one need worry about them, they are not going to fall. You can see this in what Peter said before the crucifixion, *Lord, others may deny you; (especially these other disciples of yours) but there is one man you can count on, and that's me. I'll see you through, Lord.* But the Lord said, *Thank you Peter, but before the cock crows twice you will have denied me three times* (see Mark 14:29,30). That is how much his zealous, earnest immaturity was worth!

Reluctance to Move

A third mark of childishness is an unwillingness to move on to appropriate the life and power of God which results in righteous behavior. Such a person clings instead to the initial phase of life as a baby Christian. The writer to the Hebrews puts it this way: *For though by this time you ought to be teachers* (there, it seems to me, is a measuring mark of maturity; every Christian ought to be able to teach somehow, whether or not they have a special gift of teaching), *you need some one to teach you again the first principles of God's word* (Heb. 5:12). Those first principles are the limited understanding of the word attained by new Christians or immature believers. He describes this as milk: *You need milk, not solid food; for every one who lives on milk is unskilled in the word of righteousness, for he is a child* (v. 13).

I like to think of righteousness in terms of the modern concept of "worth." Someone who is unrighteous in behavior is always so because he is not resting upon a true basis of worth imparted to him as a gift, the gift of righteousness by faith in Jesus Christ. As he grows in the knowledge of righteousness and in the awareness of his full acceptance before God, he is increasingly delivered from the need to produce a feeling of acceptance before God by works or by activities or by self-righteousness or other false ways. The writer to the Hebrews then goes on to say, in that verse we've already looked at, *But solid food* (that is, the "word of righteousness") *is for the mature, for those who have their faculties trained by practice to distinguish good from evil* (v. 14).

Now in chapter 6, which begins with the word *therefore*, there is a tie with what he has just said in chapter 5. We tend to miss this because of the unfortunate interjection of the chapter break. His word really goes on and says, *Therefore let us leave the elementary doctrines of Christ.* These are doctrines with which a new believer, still immature and understandably so, would be concerned. He lists them now: *not laying again a foundation of repentance from dead works* . . . Repentance from trying to save yourself by works before God,

134

of course, is the beginning of the Christian faith; *and of faith toward God, with instruction about ablutions* (rites such as baptism, the Lord's Supper, etc.), *the laying on of hands, the resurrection of the dead, and eternal judgment* (Heb. 6:1,2). Now all these things are initial stages, relating to the realm of children growing and learning the truth. It is a terrible thing for Christians who have been Christians for years to be still involved heavily, on an emotional level, with these elementary doctrines. They are like cases of physically arrested development—children who don't grow up—a tragic situation. Therefore, his exhortation is to leave these things and go on to maturity; that is, to the word of righteousness which is the solid food that ought to occupy the mature. The point is, a mature (or maturing) Christian ought increasingly to be concerned with manifesting the character of Christ, by seeking to be obedient to the Word of God.

Now the question comes, what about you? How much have you grown? Are you moving away from these childish attributes of instability and overconfidence? Are you growing in the faith and in the knowledge of the Son of God?

Growth does not always occur at a constant speed. The Scriptures indicate that it is discernible in stages. Did you ever watch a child growing? Parents know that growth follows a physical pattern in definite stages. A friend told me recently about his fourteen-year-old boy and the way he was shooting up into manhood. He had grown a foot in the last year. The father said that for fourteen years he had been able to wear a certain size of shoe without rivalry, but his son had suddenly developed the same size of foot and his father found him constantly borrowing his shoes. But he said, with a sigh of relief, "The last time we bought shoes for that boy, his feet had grown beyond mine. So now I am safe again." That is the way growth occurs, by stages.

We enter the Christian life as babes and may grow quite rapidly at first. Then for quite a while we may resist the great principles which make for Christian development. We are perhaps surprised to learn that God intends to do something quite different with us than we thought he would when we first became Christians. We resist these changes and do not like the way he deals with us at times, so growth slows down. But finally he brings us to the place where we give in and accept the radical principles and give ourselves to understanding them. Then we experience a new surge of growth. We feel we have at last overcome our hot tempers or our passionate natures, and we think we have learned to be easygoing, friendly, happy individuals. We give up our bitterness, our grudges, our jealousy and other ugly things. Then, to our dismay, we are put with the wrong person or into a sudden crisis and out it all comes again! We sag with discouragement and go to the Lord and say, "What's the matter, Lord? Why am I still so immature?"

Have you ever felt that way? I have, many times. But God is not through with us yet and gradually we learn how wily the flesh is and how it resists detection. Looking back we can see that we too are following the stages outlined by the apostle John as normal to Christian growth: little children, young men and fathers. We may come into a relative degree of maturity within a few years of our conversion, but we shall be engaged in the process of growth as long as we are in this present life. After all, as someone has pointed out, it takes God years to grow an oak tree, but he can grow a squash in three months. The world has seen enough of Christian squashes.

But there is a second way by which we can measure

our growth. Negatively we can mark the distance we have moved from childish attitudes, but there is a positive measurement also. Paul says, *Rather, speaking the truth in love, we are to grow up in every way* (Eph. 4:15). Previously we noted that this could be translated, "truthing in love," i.e. living the truth in love. As we have seen, it means essentially the development of honest, realistic attitudes—not a brutal frankness but a gracious loving acceptance. If this is to be manifest to others it must begin with our attitude toward ourselves. "Love thy neighbor *as thyself*" is the statement of a fundamental law of life.

Face the Failures

Maturity means a return to realism about yourself. It means to accept yourself as God accepts you: a person with certain unchangeable characteristics which God himself has given you and which therefore are advantages, no matter how much they may appear to be disadvantages to you now. These are: your physical looks, your temperament, your family and ancestry, and your mental endowments. Having all these, you now learn that as a Christian you are the dearly beloved child of a heavenly Father who is patiently teaching you to rely upon the life of his Son in you as the only resource you need to meet every demand that life can make upon you. He knows that you do not learn this easily, and he has made arrangements in advance so that no mistake or failure (deliberate or otherwise) which you make will ever in any way diminish his loving concern for you and his fatherly care over you. For your own good, however, he desires you to recognize these failures and sins for what they are and to be realistic (mature) about them, calling them exactly what he calls them. As long as you don't want to do this you will experience difficulty in realizing his undiminished love for you, because you have temporarily succumbed to the lies of an enemy. But when you realize what is happening and return to realism, honestly facing these failures for what they are, you are immediately freed to enjoy again the warmth and enrichment of his fatherly love. And once again you have fully available to you all the power to act that is inherent in the life of a resurrected Lord.

Your progress in maturity can thus be measured by the degree to which you accept the truth about yourself and others in love. That truth will be both shocking and healing. You will be shocked to learn how much you love and wish to preserve attitudes and even actions which the Scripture reveals are arising from the flesh, the old nature, which the cross of Christ has condemned *in toto*. But you will be healed and helped by understanding that you no longer have any need of those attitudes and actions to make you acceptable and loved by God, and you can now be yourself, in truth; you can live before men without pretense, having nothing to protect or hide, with no need for posturing or defensiveness. That is maturity.

There is a phenomenon which is often present among missionaries who first go out to foreign countries, called "culture shock." It happens when people find themselves plunged into a totally new situation where all the familiar cues that made them feel at ease are absent. They find themselves unable to communicate with others and thus to show them how intelligent, how valuable, they are. Especially is this true when a new language must be learned and when even after months of study one finds one's self only able to carry on a conversation at a marketplace level. It can be a most disconcerting, even shattering experience.

Among new missionaries this culture shock often manifests itself in some form of rejection. They reject the country they are in; they cannot stand anything about it, everyting is wrong. They criticize and carp and find fault with almost everything. Sometimes the rejection is leveled against the Mission Board which has sent them out. They blame the board and their fellow missionaries, saying that everything has gone wrong because they were not properly trained or prepared before they came. Sometimes the rejection is turned against themselves and they blame themselves for everything. They feel they are total misfits and failures and that they do not fit in the missionary role. Older, wiser, missionaries learn to recognize rejection as a symptom of culture shock and can often do wonders in steadying a new missionary helping him to go through this crisis safely.

Shock of Self-Discovery

Something very much like this takes place with every new Christian as well. After all, Christianity is a totally different way of living. It relies upon wholly different resources and requires quite opposite reactions than those we utilized as "natural" men. It is a form of culture shock to learn that all the familiar props to our ego are taken away from us and we are confronted with the shock of self-discovery. We learn that much of our acceptance by others was dependent upon impressions we could make but which did not correspond to any reality in us. They were poses, roles we were playing, phantoms of our imaginations.

All the ego-salving techniques which the world commonly employs and which we had previously found perfectly acceptable are now unacceptable as Christians. The tit-for-tat basis for comfortable relationships with others (you scratch my back and I'll scratch yours) is no longer to be approved. We learn we must love our enemies and do good to those who despitefully use us, and pray for those who persecute us. The effect upon others that our physical or personal attractiveness has, or the dazzling character of our personality, we now find to be totally unimpressive to the Holy Spirit. This produces a culture shock which can be terribly disconcerting and frightening. But if it be truly grasped and accepted and with it we accept the new reality of the love of a heavenly Father and the power-to-do of a living, indwelling Lord, we shall find ourselves free— free to be men and women living as God intended men and women should live when he made them in the beginning. The measure of that freedom, experienced from day to day, is the measure of our maturity.

How does one mature himself or help mature another person? That's the question every pastor, every Christian education director, anyone working in any level of Christian leadership must ask. The answer is, by developing spirituality. Spirituality is the health, the condition of the spirit which allows maturity to develop. Therefore, maturity comes by a constant endeavor to be and to live spiritually.

Paul says this very plainly in 1 Corinthians, in a great passage that deals with this matter more insightfully than perhaps anywhere else. He says: *Yet among the mature we do impart wisdom, although it is not a wisdom of this age or of the rulers of this age, who are doomed to pass away. But we impart a secret and hidden wisdom of God, which God decreed before the ages of our glorification* (1 Cor. 2:6,7). Here he is mentioning some important things. He says, first, that there are two kinds of wisdom: a *wisdom of this age* and a *secret and hidden wisdom of God*. He says that the rulers of this age—that is, the wise and important leaders of the world around us—do not understand this secret wisdom of God. They don't understand the processes of the kingdom of God and the ways people react to one another within the kingdom of God. *None of the rulers of this age understood this*, he said, *for if they had, they*

140

would not have crucified the Lord of glory (1 Cor. 2:8).

The Mind of Christ

But there is a wisdom given by the Spirit and he quotes a reference: *What no eye has seen, nor ear heard, nor the heart of man conceived, what God has prepared for those who love him, God has revealed to us through the Spirit* (vv. 9,10). The Spirit, therefore, who has given the revelation of truth in the Scriptures, has given us a secret and hidden wisdom which is designed for our glorification; that is, to lead us to the place where we're ready for glory, which is maturity. He goes on to say what this wisdom is: *For the Spirit searches everything, even the depths of God. For what person knows a man's thoughts except the spirit of the man which is in him? So also no one comprehends the thoughts of God except the Spirit of God* (vv. 10,11). Here is wisdom. The wisdom of this age is the thoughts of man, but the wisdom from above is *the thoughts of God.* He says, *Now we have received not the spirit of the world* (which is involved with the wisdom of the world), *but the Spirit which is from God, that we might understand the gifts bestowed on us by God. And we impart this in words not taught by human wisdom but taught by the Spirit, interpreting spiritual truths to those who possess the Spirit* (vv. 12,13). There is no way of understanding this kind of knowledge, the secret that makes for glorification, apart from the Spirit of God within us who teaches us these things.

He concludes the passage: *The unspiritual man does not receive the gifts of the Spirit of God, for they are folly to him, and he is not able to understand them because they are spiritually discerned. The spiritual man judges all things, but is himself to be judged by no one. "For who has known the mind of the Lord so as to instruct him?" But we have the mind of Christ* (vv. 14-

16). The spiritual man is the man who has learned by the Spirit to think and view life as Christ does; he has the mind of Christ. He has learned to see all the daily circumstances of his life as God sees them, in God's perspective. He is not, therefore, likely to be influenced by natural thinking, a view of things that the world in its non-regenerate condition would take. This is the difference between natural thinking and spiritual thinking. Spiritual thinking marks the mature man, or the spiritual man, while unspiritual thinking marks the immature, or the unspiritual, individual as a Christian. He is still a Christian but he is given to natural thinking.

Now what is this secret and hidden wisdom which Paul says is imparted for our glorification? Paul describes it very clearly in Colossians in the close of the first chapter, where he is speaking again about maturity. In Colossians 1:26 he says the secret wisdom of God is *the mystery hidden for ages and generations but now made manifest to his saints. To them*, he says, speaking especially of the Gentiles, *God chose to make known how great among the Gentiles are the riches of the glory of this mystery* (now here it is, here's the mystery), *which is Christ in you, the hope of glory*. It is the mystery of being saved by the death of Christ, but living by his life in us. His life reproduced in us is the mystery that results in maturity and the secret of spirituality. Being spiritual is living on the basis of Christ at work within us.

Him we proclaim, Paul continues, *warning every man and teaching every man in all wisdom, that we may present every man mature in Christ* (Col. 1:28). Maturity comes as we grow in understanding this secret of how to live by his life in us. Paul adds, *For this I toil, striving with all the energy which he mightily inspires within me* (v. 29). That is, his own maturity comes from this source. He is able to bring others to maturity.

Joined and Knit Together

Even as we come to understand this, however, we must always bear in mind that we are members of the body of Christ. In the closing lines of the passage we have been looking at in Ephesians, the apostle mentions one further thing which is of great importance. He says that this growth into maturity takes place within the context of . . . *the whole body, joined and knit together by every joint with which it is supplied, when each part is working properly* (Eph. 4:16). Paul here says that one of the factors that makes for growth in maturity is to accept the ministry of other Christians to yourself. The parts of the body are designed to meet one another's needs—they are *joined and knit together*. The apostle actually coins a word to express the mutual ministry of members of the body to each other. The word for "joined" is made up of three Greek words: one is the root from which we get our English word "harmony"; another is the word "with"; and the third is the word for "choosing." His idea is that the honest yet loving ministry of Christian to Christian issues in continual choices made in harmony, so that the end result is a witness before the world that increases the body numerically and strengthens it spiritually.

It means, therefore, that you are where you are because that is where God wants you. He put you with the Christians around you because they are the kind you need and you are the kind they need. They may be rather prickly and thorny and hard to live with, but they are what you need at the present time. As each member of the body accepts this and ministers to one another in honesty and love, each one doing what he is equipped to do, there will emerge a marvelous harmony which makes for maturity in the whole body.

Do not reject God's instruments. He knows what you

need better than you do. Do not struggle with the place in which he has put you. Accept it, welcome it, and seek to relate in honest love to other Christians around you. There will be pain at times but through the pain will come growth. As you go on, remember that day by day, hour by hour, moment by moment, the Spirit of God is working a miracle. Individual Christians are growing into the manhood of Jesus Christ and the whole body together is manifesting more and more clearly before a watching world the wholesome, balanced, well-adjusted, capable, manhood of the stature of Jesus Christ.

CHAPTER TWELVE

Impact

What happens when a church in the twentieth century begins to operate on these principles? Will they work today as they did in the early church? The answer is a resounding Yes! When Jesus said, *Upon this rock I will build my church; and the gates of hell shall not prevail against it* (Matt. 16:18, *KJV*), he had all the centuries in view until his return. Dr. E. M. Blaiklock, Professor of Classics at Auckland University in New Zealand, has said, "Of all the centuries, the twentieth is most like the first." Once again, Christians are a small minority in the midst of a despairing and pagan world, and they are confronted on every side with violence, hostility, ignorance, widespread immorality, and existential despair. They are thus thrust back into the very climate of the first century where the events and triumphs of the book of Acts occurred.

As we have seen, the Christianity of the book of Acts is not unusual Christianity—it is normal, usual, typical Christianity as it was designed to be. The sterile formal, doctrinaire Christianity of our times is the distortion, with its coldness, its narrow rigidity, its perfunctory ritual, and its bland conformity. Every century has had its distorted forms of Christianity, but every century has likewise known something, at least, of the vital transforming power of Jesus Christ at work through his body. That power has been manifested in the twentieth century also, strongly at certain times and places, much more weakly elsewhere, depending on the degree to which individual churches have either deliberately or unwittingly conformed to the biblical pattern of operation we have been discovering.

To Manifest Life

Perhaps it will be helpful to summarize that pattern in one or two paragraphs that it may be clearly before us. The church is here on earth, not to do what other groups can do, but to do what no other group of human beings can possibly do. It is here to manifest the life and power of Jesus Christ in fulfillment of the ministry which was given him by the Father, as he quoted it himself in the synagogue at Nazareth. *The Spirit of the Lord is upon me . . . to preach good news to the poor . . . to proclaim release to the captives and recovering of sight to the blind, to set at liberty those who are oppressed, to proclaim the acceptable year of the Lord* (Luke 4:18,19).

That healing ministry is to be carried out through the activity of many, not just a few. It takes the whole church to do the work of the church. To this end every

146

Christian is endowed with certain gifts which were promised by the resurrected Christ when he ascended on high to the Father's throne and took over the reins of the universe. The supreme task of every Christian's life is to discover his gift and put it to work. If anyone does not do this the whole body will suffer.

The power by which these gifts are to be operative is that of a continual reliance upon the imparted life of an indwelling, resurrected Lord. Further, full provision has been made for the discovery, development, and operation of these spiritual gifts in resurrection power through the moulding ministry of apostles, prophets (who lay the foundations of faith), and evangelists and pastor-teachers (who use the word of God to motivate, cleanse, and strengthen the people to their tasks). In the doing of all this, the church will find itself operating as salt and light in the midst of a world of corruption and darkness, and at the same time it will itself be growing into an increasing manifestation of the wholeness and beauty of the humanity of Jesus Christ. That is the whole program.

With considerable reluctance I now turn to the experience of a single church in order to demonstrate from real life how well these principles do in fact work in this modern world. The church I have in mind is the one in which I have been privileged to be a pastor-teacher since 1950. It is the Peninsula Bible Church, located on the San Francisco peninsula, at Palo Alto, California. I am fully aware that there are many other churches in the world which could serve as illustrations of the principles we have studied, and doubtless some of them would be much clearer and better examples than the Peninsula Bible Church. But my limited experience forces me to write only of the church I know best, known familiarly to its members as PBC.

I must also make clear at the outset that by no

means is PBC a perfect church. We have made many mistakes through the years and some of them have been grievous indeed. We are still very much learners, being led along by the Holy Spirit into continually unfolding vistas and clearer understanding of the principles we seek to follow. We have learned much from the experience and teaching of others, and feel most keenly our debt to members of the body elsewhere for their •deeply needed ministry to us. Compared to many other churches around we have found what many regard as an enviable plateau of success; but compared to the New Testament standard, we often fall very far short, and can perhaps be best described by the word of Jesus to the church at Philadelphia in Asia Minor: *Behold, I have set before you an open door, which no one is able to shut; I know that you have but little power, and yet you have kept my word and have not denied my name* (Rev. 3:8).

PBC was begun by five businessmen in 1948, who, with their families, felt the need for a warmer time of informal fellowship and Bible study than they were obtaining in the churches they were then attending. They did not have any intention whatsoever of beginning a new church, but merely wished to supplement the spiritual diet they were getting. To do this they rented a small room in the Palo Alto Community Center and began holding Sunday evening meetings, while they were still attending their own churches in the mornings. It is now possible to look back and see that what they were hungering for was the *koinonia*, the body life, of the early church. This they achieved to a considerable degree and the meetings were so warm and enjoyable that they attracted many others who dropped in regularly for the Bible teaching (often by visiting pastors) and the songfests and informal atmosphere.

So acceptable was this ministry that at the end of

one year the people approached the five leaders and asked if they would consider having a Sunday morning Sunday School, as well as the evening meeting, since their children needed the biblical instruction which the parents were receiving in the evenings. This was done, and by the fall of 1950 the number of regular attendants, both adults and children, was running around 100 each week. This was more demanding than the five leaders could handle in the limited time available to them, and thus, in September of 1950, through some rather obvious leading of the Lord, I was privileged to come to the group as their first, full-time pastor.

Of all the principles we have discussed in this book, the only one clear to me at the time of my arrival was deep conviction, derived from Ephesians 4, that the work of the ministry belonged to the people and not to the pastor. I was rather vague as to what that ministry was, but felt from the first that my task as pastor was to unfold the word of God in its fullness, as best I could understand it, and leave to laymen the major responsibility for visitation of the sick, presiding at and leading church services, and evangelizing the world. We determined from the start that we would do no direct evangelizing in the regular services of the church, or within the church building, but all evangelization would be done in homes, backyards, rented halls or other public meeting places.

Deliberately Low-Key

One of the prominent features of our earlier days was the ministry of Home Bible Classes. These were aimed, not at teaching Christians, but at interesting non-Christians in the great themes of the gospel. They were deliberately low-keyed in approach, with a total absence of activities with a churchy flavor, such as hymn-singing, opening prayer, chairs lined up in rows, use of a lectern, etc. The host and hostess were key figures, opening their home to friends and guests whom they welcomed and made to feel at home as though this were a purely social occasion. A lay teacher taught from the Bible, seeking to capture the biblical concepts and express them in contemporary terms, and then discussion was invited, with no holds barred. Anyone was free to challenge what was presented if they cared to, and their challenges were listened to carefully and courteously and an answer was sought from the Scriptures themselves.

These meetings were an instant success and became so popular that the discussions would sometimes involve scores and even hundreds of people (we had some very large homes available) and would go on at times to the wee hours of the morning. No mention was ever made of PBC at these home meetings for they were regarded as the personal ministry of the Christians involved. There were soon many new converts coming from these classes, who were then urged to become active in a local church, preferably one close to them. Thus the whole body of Christ in our area began to profit from these classes, and naturally many of the new converts ended up at PBC.

Looking back we can now see that these classes accomplished three very important ends. Once, they proved a most effective tool to reach worldlings right where they were, and to introduce them personally and directly to the Lord of glory who had come into the world to call the lost, and not the righteous, to repentance. Second, they afforded visible demonstration to our Christian people that the gospel still had power to transform lives, and was tremendously attractive to non-Christians when it was presented without all the religious trappings of a church service. Third, it gave many Christians an opportunity to become personally the channel of God's Spirit at work, and thus filled them with excitement and adventurous anticipation. Their turned-on lives became a spark to others, and gradually the excitement of vital Christianity began to spread. In this threefold way the Home Bible Class ministry overcame what we learned to call "the huddle syndrome" among Christians, that is, the tendency to group together in the presence of non-Christians or to avoid anything but the most superficial contact with worldlings, especially avoiding close friendships or extensive hospitality with such. When Christians recovered their confidence in the power of the gospel, they lost their fear of the world, and now this has pervaded the whole church to the extent that we do not need a group approach to witnessing nearly as much as before, and most witnessing and evangelizing is done now on a personal basis through friendship and hospitality evangelism.

One of the five founding businessmen became so skilled in developing his spiritual gifts of teaching, discernment, and leadership that three other elders invited him to become a full-time pastor, and thus Mr. Robert W. Smith began his rich and varied ministry with PBC as associate pastor without the benefit of the usual full seminary training often thought essential. Later Mr. David Roper became an Associate Pastor with responsibility to utilize the same principles of ministry outlined in Ephesians 4 within the college community. He has so successfully applied these that the Christian witness on nearby Stanford University campus is, in my judgment, the most effective that I know of on any campus in the world.

The same pattern of approach has been found eminently workable at the high school level, and the coming of Mr. Ronald Ritchie to the pastoral staff in 1969 corresponded with the outbreak of the "Jesus movement" on the West Coast, giving us an opportunity to apply these principles with such widespread results that literally hundreds of high school young people were baptized as new converts to Jesus Christ. So vital was their Christian commitment and interest that they have reached out all over northern California and beyond, to share their growing maturity and stability in Christ.

Church Within a Church

One of the most significant developments resulting from an application of these principles is the Career Class which meets in a restaurant every Sunday morning. This single-adult group — over 400 strong — is a church within a church. It is operated by unanimous decision arrived at through prayer within its own steering committee and it is pastored by Ron Ritchie and a large staff of lay teachers. The needs of single adults are being met, so these people are learning to be available to one another as brothers and sisters and to put aside the world's concepts of how single men and women ought to regard one another and themselves. This class is a real bridge into the community, as many disillusioned, bored or broken people find their way to the informal, lively meetings. Through the straightforward presentation of the truth of the gospel, many are finding their way to Christ and discovering that they are then part of a loving, supportive family and their joy quickly reproduces itself in others.

It may surprise many to learn that these same principles of ministry will work with Christians of any age or background, even with children. We have found that junior high and even junior age children are capable of discovering and exercising their spiritual gifts, and of learning how to rely on resurrection power to make it all effective. As a consequence, junior high young people are helping teach younger children with great

152

effect, and every summer teams of youngsters are sent out, with adult leadership, to hold week-long meetings for children in remote towns and villages of California, Oregon, and Nevada. Beside the fruit this ministry bears in the lives of many spiritually neglected children in these little towns, is the effect the ministry itself has in the lives of those who go. They learn great lessons of trust and of the faithfulness of God, since they do all the planning and conducting of the meetings that are held.

It is difficult, in one brief chapter, to describe all the varied ministries that have developed in the past few years as individual Christians in our congregation have fallen into line with the biblical pattern of the Spirit's working. Three others must be mentioned, since they illustrate so well the innovative quality of the Spirit's direction, bringing into being approaches and techniques which have not been done before or which were never planned or expected. Serendipity is inevitable when a creative Spirit is at work.

Interns and Scribes

For instance, there is the intern training program at PBC now operated under the name Discovery Center. This grew out of the concern of the pastoral staff to do something to fill the lack of practical ministry for seminary students during summers. The academic pressures and climate of seminary made it difficult for young ministerial students to put to work some of the principles they were learning, and so PBC undertook to bring one or two young men each summer to work with the staff in outreach ministry. These young men were soon found to be seriously lacking in three major areas of scriptural understanding: the spiritual walk of an individual in reliance on resurrection power; the understanding of spiritual gifts and how the body of Christ functions; and the position and power of the church in relationship to society and social problems.

For summer after summer these concepts were taught to young seminarians, with PBC bearing the expense of their ministry, involving a monthly salary of $250 for single students, and $300 per month for married. The number varied from two to a maximum of twelve one particular summer. Then young people began coming to us and saying, "We've heard of your training program and we want to get in on it. We will come for a year or so, and pay our own expenses, if you will let us join this program." We discouraged this at first, feeling it would put too much strain upon the pastoral staff, but several were so persistent that we made a venture and took two young people on for one year. When word of this got out we were flooded with applicants, and finally were forced either to make due provision for this or abandon it entirely. We went ahead, trusting God to lead, and thus began our internship program.

Out of that program, which continued for five years, evolved what is now called Scribe School. Scribes are chosen from applicants in all age groups and from varied backgrounds who desire to learn how to teach the Scriptures. For two years, they are plunged into the Greek and Hebrew languages, guided in the discovery of practical teaching skills and introduced to matters of theology and church history. They maintain a close association with individual pastors in a tutorial capacity. Scribes, unlike interns, work at regular jobs to maintain their own support.

Still another development that was never planned or promoted but grew from small beginnings is that of Discovery Publications. This began with the interest of a young graduate student in geology at Stanford, Mr. Peter Irish, who found his eyes opened to fundamental

154

realities through a series of sermons preached on Ephesians 6, entitled "Spiritual Warfare." He determined to make these available in printed form for the benefit of others, and on his own organized a group of volunteers to copy off tapes of the messages, edit them, type them on stencils, and run off mimeographed copies. These proved so popular he was encouraged to treat other sermonic series in the same manner, and eventually found it necessary to devote his full time to this work. By word of mouth the messages were advertised and slowly a large mailing list was built up, till now over 2000 copies of each message are mailed out several times a year all over the world, beside those available to the congregation directly. These are now printed, instead of mimeographed, and include a catalog of messages in stock which cover large areas of the Scriptures, as well as many topical studies of great practical importance, such as studies on sex, marriage, family relationships, war, the occult, etc.

The third area of unique development is that of the Sunday evening Body Life service. This has attracted so much attention that several Christian magazines have made mention of it and one, *Christianity Today*, ran a special column describing the meeting, in their issue of May 21, 1971. By special permission of the magazine, we will close this chapter with that description.

It happens every Sunday night. Eight hundred or more people pack into a church auditorium designed to seat comfortably only 750. Seventy per cent are under twenty-five, but adults of all ages, even into the eighties, are mingled with the youth, and people of widely varying cultural backgrounds all sit, sing, and pray together.

A leader stands at the center front, a microphone around his neck. "This is the family," he says. "This is the body of Christ. We need each other. You have spiritual gifts which I need, and I have some that you need. Let's share with each other." When a hand goes up toward the back of the center section a red-haired youth runs down the center aisle with a wireless microphone. It is passed down the pew to the young man, who stands waiting to speak. "Man, I don't know how to start," he says, his shoulder-length hair shining as he turns from side to side. "All I know is that I've tried the sex trip and the drug trip and all the rest but it was strictly nowhere. But last week I made the Jesus trip—or I guess I should say that He found me—and man, what love! I can't get over it. I'm just a new Christian, but man, this is where it's at!" A wave of delight sweeps the auditorium, and everyone claps and smiles as the leader says "Welcome to the family. What's your name?"

Other hands are waving for recognition. The leader points to a well-groomed, attractive woman in her mid-thirties. "I just wanted to tell you of the Lord's supply to me this week," she says into the mike. She is a divorcee with small children. Her income had dwindled to the point that she'd had only forty-two cents to eat on that week. But unsolicited food had come. The family had eaten plenty, and she wants to share her thanksgiving. Another enthusiastic round of applause.

Then a sensitive-faced girl with waist-long hair: "I just want the family to pray with me. My brother's blowing his mind with LSD, and it's killing me to watch him coming apart, but we can't get him to stop."

"Phil, go over and stand by her and lead us all in prayer for this real need," the leader requests. "You were on LSD, you know how it feels." A tall, thin youth with a scraggly beard crosses to the girl, takes the mike. "O Father," he prays, "you know how Ann feels and you know how her brother feels. Show him the way out, through Jesus, and show him that you love him just the way he is." He goes on, his prayer eloquent in its simple earnestness, the whole audience listening quietly, with bowed heads.

Then a clean-cut college boy is on his feet, his Bible in his hand. "I just want to share something the Lord showed me this week." For five minutes he expounds a verse from the first letter of John, and the crowd laughs with delight at his practical application.

Other needs are shared. One blonde youth asks for prayer that he might be able to buy a car cheaply so he won't have to depend on hitch-hiking to get to his college classes on time. When the prayer is finished, a middle-aged housewife stands at the back and says, "I don't know how this happened, but just this week the Lord gave me a car I don't need. If Ernie wants it, here are the keys."

She holds up a ring of keys, and the crowd applauds joyously as the boy runs to pick up the keys.

Then an offering is announced. The leader explains that all may give as they are able, but if anyone has immediate need he is welcome to take from the plate as much as ten dollars to meet that need. If he needs more than ten, he is warmly invited to come to the church office the next morning and explain the need; more money would be available there. While ushers pass the plate, a young man with a guitar sings a folk song that asks, "Have you seen Jesus my Lord? He's there in plain view. Take a look, open your eyes, we'll show him to you."

After the song someone calls out a hymn number, and everyone stands to sing it together. Then the teacher for the evening takes over. There is a rustle of turning pages as hundreds of Bibles are opened. For perhaps twenty-five minutes the teacher speaks, pacing the platform, Bible in hand. He illustrates with simple human incidents, some humorous, some sobering. The crowd is with him all the way, looking up references, underlining words, writing in the margins. A few hands are raised with questions on the study. The teacher answers briefly or refers the question to an elder or pastor in the congregation. Then the people stand for a closing prayer. They join hands across the aisles and sing softly, "We are one in the Spirit, we are one in the Lord."

When the meeting is dismissed, few leave. They break up i..to spontaneous groups: some praying, some rapping about a Bible passage, some singing quietly with a guitar, some just visiting and sharing with one another. Gradually the crowd thins down, but it is a good hour or more before everyone is gone and the lights are turned out.

The gathering is called a Body Life Service, a time for members of the body of Christ to fulfill the function of edifying one another in love. It began in January of 1970 when the pastoral staff of Peninsula Bible Church met to discuss the spiritual status of the church. Concern was expressed about the Sunday evening service, which at that time followed a conventional pattern of song service, announcements, Scripture, special music, and preaching. Attendance was rather sparse, running about 150-250 with only a handful of youth present. The major concern was whether we were fulfilling the admonition of Scripture to "bear one an-

other's burden, and so fulfill the law of Christ."
Other texts haunted us, such as, "Confess your
faults one to another and pray for one another
that you may be healed, [admonish] one another
in psalms and hymns and spiritual songs." Where
was this occurring among our people? Where
could it occur?

We determined to make a place for this ministry by wiping out the traditional structure of the
evening service and using the time to invite a
sharing of needs and gifts by the people. We
began with the question, "Where are you hurting?
Not where did you hurt ten years ago, but now,
where are you right now?"

Predictably, it was slow getting started, but
soon a climate of honest realism began to prevail.
When that was noised abroad, without any particular invitation youth began to appear—many
long-haired, barefoot, and in bizarre dress. Our
middle-class saints gulped at first but were determined to be genuinely Christian. They welcomed
the young people, listened to them, prayed with
them, and opened their hearts. The kids did likewise.

The numbers increased by leaps and bounds.
For over a year now it has been going on with no
sign of a let-up. Every service is different. Love,
joy, and a sense of acceptance prevail so strongly
that awed visitors frequently remark about a spiritual atmosphere they can almost scoop up in their
hands. *Koinonia* has come![1]

That is part of the impact of one church which has
begun to operate on the principles of ministry found in
Ephesians 4. Other churches, elsewhere, are experienc-

1. Ray C. Stedman, "The Minister's Workshop," *Christianity Today,*
Vol. XV, May 21, 1971.

ing similar blessing, though the emphasis varies from place to place because of regional and cultural differences. Wherever a church is ready to take Ephesians 4, 1 Corinthians 12 and Romans 12 seriously, the Lord of the church is ready to heal and to bless.

Pastor Ray C. Stedman believes his task is to unfold the Word of God in its fullness. "But," claims Stedman, "the work of the ministry in the church belongs to the people."

"Please pray for my friend—she's about ready to accept Christ." Someone nearby will pray immediately. Personal requests and victories are freely expressed.

Discussing Scripture with an old friend—or new—comes naturally to those who share the warmth of Body Life.

A young man sings, "Have you seen Jesus my Lord? He's there in plain view. Take a look . . . we'll show him to you."

Collegians from PBC share their growing maturity and stability in Christ at Bible studies on Stanford campus.

People get personally involved with their Bibles at Body Life. New insights are often recorded during the study.

The warmth, informal fellowship and Bible study which characterized the first five families still reflect PBC.

When the meeting is over, few leave. Some pray, some rap about a Bible passage, some just visit and share.

Body Life Revisited

The Sunday evening Body Life service at PBC was born as the decade of the violent sixties faded into history and the more hopeful year of 1970 came into being. At a New Year's Eve service, held till midnight December 31, 1969, the sharing of the people was so warm and moving that the pastoral staff, meeting the next week, asked themselves, "Why can't we have meetings like this all the time? How can we perpetuate this beautiful spirit of love and mutual ministry?" Out of those questions a determination grew to have a service where the people could bear one another's burdens and confess their sins and pray for one another as the Scripture commanded. The latter part of chapter 12 describes such a service as it was in early 1971.

But what is it like now, six years later, in the late fall of 1976 when this is being written? Many have asked if the Body Life service was still going on and if so, in what ways has it changed? The Jesus movement has now ended or at least passed into a quieter phase where it is not as vocal and visible as it once was. Was Body Life merely a fad, passing away like many other colorful aspects of the early seventies? Have the services dwindled in attendance? Have the youth stayed on? More important, has the quality of love, once so vividly manifest, continued to be evident—or has it, too, gone the way of all flesh? These are the questions many are asking and we shall seek to answer them in this chapter.

To begin with, the services are still going on. Every Sunday evening between 6:30 P.M. and the opening time of 7:00, long lines of cars wait to turn into the parking lots. The proportions of youth to those over twenty-five have probably risen a bit, to roughly eighty percent under twenty-five, twenty percent over. The adult portion still includes men and women of all ages, some well into their sixties and seventies. A fair number of visitors are always present, on occasion representing as high as ten percent of the total congregation. Attendance remains almost constant—on rare occasions dropping to 750-800, but usually in the 900-1000 range. The service is still totally unadvertised and the elders have still thought it wise not even to mention in the church bulletin what the subject for the evening teaching will be or who will be leading, lest attendance be stimulated beyond what the facilities can handle.

One noticeable change has been in the music. The guitar still reigns as king, but the hard-driving rock bands of the early seventies are seldom ever heard. The folk rock songs of John Fischer, Marge Snyder and

Pam Marks are still popular, but the church hymnbook is used much more now and some of the great old hymns of the church are now favorites.

The teaching period is still central to the whole service. A panel of skilled and capable teachers (many of them in their late twenties or early thirties) has been developed and the Scriptures are expounded regularly with great interest and effect. More and more often the sharing period is being spontaneously tied to the passage expounded and a very practical ministry of application and exhortation grows out of the teaching time.

The sharing time itself is still the most distinctive feature of the Body Life service. Almost always it is this which either gives to all who attend a consciousness of love and deep concern or fails to give it, depending on whether the sharing is deep and genuine, or shallow and artificial. The thirty to forty minutes devoted to this at each service is never adequate for the number of those who want to share. When the leader recognizes an individual out of the number of hands raised, a wireless microphone immediately brought to him makes it possible for everyone to hear all that is said. The leader retains a live mike for himself in order to enter into dialogue, if necessary, with the one sharing. All types of needs, both spiritual and material, are shared and each one is prayed for and often on-the-spot arrangements are made to meet the needs expressed.

Because this sharing time does more than anything else to convey to all present the reality of the church as the body of Christ, it is also (along with the teaching ministry) under sharp and subtle attack from the enemy. Many churches who have attempted Body Life services have found them to take off with a roar, but soon simmer down to a degree of sameness (and dullness) and finally peter out without a whimper. The reason is largely because sharing has been allowed to follow its own course without adequate leadership or guidance and so the enemy has managed to destroy it without a struggle.

It is, of course, the business of leadership to lead. The experience of years has taught us that the key to a successful Body Life service is largely in the hands of the emcee of the meeting. He is to be far more than simply a conductor, keeping everything in order while allowing the meeting to take whatever course it will. He must, in addition, be aware of what will eventually kill the spirit of a service and be very sensitive to recognize those dangerous trends when they begin and to move with graciousness and yet firmness to eliminate them. The delicate balance between sensitive leadership and the autocratic hand of overcontrol, is something only the Spirit of God can produce, but it is an absolute essential to a continuing and fruitful Body Life service.

Within the first year of conducting a Body Life service we came to recognize three factors which are guaranteed to kill the service within a very short time if allowed to go unchallenged. These factors crop up continuously. One or two appearances can be allowed to pass without danger, but they seem to be very infectious and, if not halted by the leadership, will soon take over the sharing and turn the meeting into dull unreality.

The first of these we call "superficial sharing." It refers to sharing trivial matters rather than the real burdens with which people are wrestling. To ask people to pray for nice weather for a fishing trip or that you might find your lost pencil or to get a good grade on a test is to misuse the purpose of Body Life sharing. The same passage which bids us to *bear one another's burdens* (Gal. 6:2) goes on in 6:5 to say, *For every man shall bear his own burden (KJV)*. Two different words are used for *burden* in this context. The first one means a burden of great weight, too heavy for anyone to carry alone. The second use refers to a much smaller load which any healthy person should be able to handle without help.

Superficial sharing usually occurs when an individual is afraid to risk anything of real depth. It can arise from pride, which seeks to maintain status and does not wish to appear weak or a failure. It can come from fear that whatever is shared will be met with condemnation or rejection or that it will make him a laughingstock. Or it can come from a lightweight view of life that regards every little problem as the legitimate concern of the whole body. Whatever the cause, it is the business of the leader to discern what lies behind the symptom of superficial sharing and to give instruction that will make possible a true and proper sharing of real burdens. We have found that one of the helpful things a leader can do is to ask the question: "Where do you hurt?" True burdens are those that cause real hurts, and that is what is meant to be covered by the exhortation, *Bear one another's burdens.*

Somewhat similar to superficial sharing and the second factor that is guaranteed to kill a Body Life service, is what can be termed "secondary sharing." Since the sharing of personal hurts is apparently risky to many, they find they can still participate by sharing someone else's burden. "Please pray for my Aunt Mary in Florida. She has just found out that she has cancer and is very frightened of death." This, of course, is a perfectly legitimate source of concern but it is the kind of concern which every person present probably has, and if they all began to share other people's hurts there would be no bearing of their own burdens.

Sometimes, of course, the one voicing such a concern is so intimately involved with the one for whom prayer

173

is requested or is torn himself by the burden the other bears that such a request represents a legitimate burden. Often our emcees will ask someone who shares another's burden, "How is this affecting you? Do you feel hurt by this threat to your friend's welfare?" When the individual's personal concern is voiced, the subsequent prayer includes both the need described and the one who voiced it. It is not always easy to distinguish between legitimate burdens for others in desperate need and the use of such to avoid sharing one's own pressing hurt. But Body Life leaders must understand that once secondary sharing starts it is difficult to stop, and yet if allowed to continue it will move the meeting toward dullness and sterility.

The third area of danger is that of "inadequate response." The first, most needed, and yet easiest response to give to a burden shared is to pray for it. This should always be done and preferably by someone who can identify with the problem or need or who has gone through it himself. Prayer must never be permitted to degenerate to shallow and cliché-ridden response. The Apostle James outlines such an instance: *Suppose a brother or sister is without clothes and daily food. If one of you says to him, "Go, I wish you well; keep warm and well fed," but does nothing about his physical needs, what good is it?* (Jas. 2:15,16, *NIV*). In such an instance, even to add "I will pray for you" is hardly a cut better than the answer James records. Such a situation requires action—now!

At PBC we often get requests for help in finding jobs, counsel in overcoming bad habits, need for physical help in moving or meeting some extra demand, requests for financial assistance, etc., etc. To simply pray for these and pass on to some other request is almost insulting. A sincere effort must be made to go further. Here the total resources of the total body must be called into

174

play. Nothing is more exciting than to see how quickly such needs can be met when the whole body is invited to participate. We have seen jobs provided right on the spot; doctor's services donated; financial counselling arranged for; cars given to those without transportation; unmarried mothers-to-be taken into homes till their babies come; alcoholics and drug addicts given help; many food supplies given; baby-sitting services supplied for working mothers, and so on. To actually see these needs being met right before their eyes gives to everyone present a sense of excitement and of the reality of Christian love and concern. Care must always be taken that none of these responses be abused or over-indulged, but it is the duty of elders to exercise just such care and nothing will deliver an elder more surely from business-as-usual blahs than to experience involvement in the human stream of need and care.

Though the Body Life service itself is still vital, real, and deeply involved with human need, as the preceding paragraphs describe, still by far the greatest effect it has is to stimulate and encourage such living all through the week and throughout the entire body of Christ. Christians are to be loving, caring, thoughtful servants of others—not merely at a Body Life service once a week, but at all times, wherever they are. We seek to remind everyone of this at the Body Life service. It has been most encouraging to see how the spirit of Body Life sharing has spread throughout the body and is practiced frequently through the week. No mention of these experiences is likely to be made, but the God who sees in secret takes note of all and is faithful to remember these labors of love with unusual and unexpected blessing.

How long will the Body Life service continue? We have no way of knowing. If it continues to meet genuine human needs in true Christian love and concern, avoiding the shallow, the superficial and the inadequate response, there is no reason why it should not go on till the Lord returns. If it fails to do so, but degenerates into a mere form, kept alive only by artificial programming and great organizational effort, it would be better to let it die and to allow people to feel its lack till their spirit turns to the Lord in bored desperation and cries out for renewal and healing.

Some Problems Faced

Doubtless many questions will be raised by this study. As I have met pastors and concerned laymen from place to place they have often asked perceptive and practical questions about how these scriptural principles might be put to work in a local church, under varying conditions. The questions many have asked and the answers I have given are reproduced below with the hope they may help many who read this book.

Q. "In a church which has for years followed a more conventional approach, where should a pastor begin to implement these concepts?"

A. The proper place to begin is with an exposition of the Scriptures, from the pulpit, over a period of time, to help the church see that the Bible does teach these things, and that they have behind them the weight of biblical authority. The pastor must be gracious and loving, not lashing at his people, but gently leading them to the place where they will be ready to change.

Q. "What can be done by laymen when a pastor resists these scriptural principles and refuses to consider them?"

A. This is a delicate situation, though unfortunately it is met all too frequently. Perhaps a church board can send its pastor to a conference where these principles are taught, or ask him to meet with other pastors who have experienced these concepts at work; or perhaps a copy of this book may help him. A thoughtful and patient approach will usually work wonders in this type of a situation.

Q. "If these principles are so clearly taught in Scripture, how come I was not taught them in seminary?"

A. That is a difficult question to answer. It is easy for a seminary to begin to train men to fit what the churches are looking for, rather than to hold closely to the biblical pattern. Tradition is a powerful force, and seminaries, like individuals, can succumb to the pressure to conform. In the course of church history, it is the seminaries which are reformed by the spiritual awakenings among the churches, rather than vice versa. Many seminaries are moving strongly toward renewed emphasis on these biblical principles.

Q. "I agree that what you've presented is scriptural, but it demands tremendous motivation to get a congregation moving in this direction. How do you supply this?"

A. Motivation can come from three sources: an awareness of the desperate condition of the church today;

the hungering of individuals after excitement and challenge in ministry; and the conviction, arising from the Scriptures, that God will act as he has said. Try a bit of all three.

Q. "How would you recommend that we start a Body Life service?"

A. First, do not try to borrow a few techniques of leadership and expect the service to go. A Body Life service must emerge from the deep conviction of a congregation that they have a responsibility before the Lord to "bear one another's burdens." They must be helped to see the need for sharing, for honesty, and for mutual acceptance. When they respond to these with conviction, then it is time to try a Body Life service. Keep the service as simple as possible, and above all, don't over-organize or attempt to manipulate it.

Q. "Are you not afraid that exhibitionists will take advantage of such a service to relate sordid or scandalous matters?"

A. Despite the openness of Body Life services at PBC, nothing like this has occurred. If it did, the leadership would welcome it as an opportunity to teach the congregation what certain types of problem require in the way of sharing, and perhaps ask the individual involved to meet with a pastor or elder afterward. If this is done graciously, it will turn an embarrassing moment into a tremendous teaching and learning experience.

Q. "Is it not unwise to share your innermost secrets with other people? Isn't it better to keep them entirely to oneself?"

A. No, it is not better to keep them to yourself. Christians are explicitly instructed to bear one another's burdens, and are equipped, through various spiritual gifts, to do so. Of course, some selectivity should be observed as to the trustworthiness of those with whom one shares, and certainly deep dark secrets should not be aired publicly, but no Christian should have to struggle on alone, wrestling with some terrible habit or overwhelming situation. He is cheating himself of the help of the rest of the body if he does not share with someone.

Q. "What spiritual gifts should I have to be a pastor?"

A. Of course you should have the gift of a pastor-teacher. This is fundamental. It is manifested by a compassion toward those in need, and an ability to teach the Scriptures in such a way as to see people delivered by truth. Other gifts are helpful, such as: gifts of wisdom and knowledge, discernment, prophecy, showing mercy, and the gift of faith.

Q. "Should all our Sunday School teachers have the gift of teaching?"

A. By all means! Sunday School teachers should not be selected because they are willing, or because no one else will do it. They should show some ability to improve the spiritual life of others through teaching before they are entrusted with a class. Molding the lives of young people through teaching is far too important to trust it to the unqualified.

Q. "What if a congregation is so small that it does not have qualified teachers for the Sunday School?"

A. Then it would be much better to have the children taught at home by their parents. Also, the Scripture instructs a church to *pray the Lord of the harvest that he might thrust forth laborers into the harvest field* (see Matt. 9:38). We have filled many a vacancy in our Sunday School by this method.

Q. "Is it wrong to give an invitation in a church service?"

A. It is not a question of being wrong but rather of being inappropriate. There are occasions when it is most appropriate, if done graciously and sincerely, without undue emotional appeal. But in general it tends to weaken a church to make this a continual practice, for time must then be taken from the work of equipping the saints unto the work of the ministry. There is very little time available for this anyhow in the usual church service and that is surely a far more important matter when the makeup of the congregation is essentially Christian.

Q. "How long will it take to get a congregation operating on Ephesians 4 principles?"

A. That depends entirely on the individual congregation and its pastor or pastors. It will probably take much longer than one would at first think, for Christians often require much thought and time before they accept new approaches. But if only a few in a congregation catch on and start exercising their spiritual gifts in resurrection power, it will be a spark that will ignite others and gradually pronounced change can occur. Remember, *The Lord's servant must not be quarrelsome but kindly to every one, an apt teacher, forbearing, correcting his opponents with gentleness* (2 Tim. 2:24).

Q. "Is there any word of encouragement you can say to a pastor who is just beginning to put the principles you expound to work?"

A. Yes. Here it is. *Tend the flock of God that is your charge, not by constraint but willingly, not for shameful gain but eagerly, not as domineering over those in* *your charge but being examples to the flock. And when the chief Shepherd is manifested you will obtain the unfading crown of glory* (1 Pet. 5:2-4).

BODY LIFE IS

SHARING
GROWING
GIVING
DISCOVERING

... TOGETHER

A **Study Guide** is available for use with this book. The **Body Life Study Guide,** for individual or group study, includes helps for leaders. Learning activities involve every member of the study group and include programmed instruction, agree/disagree sheets, inductive Bible study, definition of scriptural concepts, and sharing activities. For use with high school through adult.